WINDOW SILL GARDENING

WINDOW SILL GARDENING

JAMES UNDERWOOD CROCKETT

An American Garden Guild Book
DOUBLEDAY & COMPANY, INC.
GARDEN CITY, NEW YORK
1958

TO MARGARET

Contents

6   Contents

4 Contents

List of Illustrations

WORDS OF ENCOURAGEMENT

Every plant we think of as a house plant has relatives living at this very moment in some part of the world without human help at all. Some grow as abundantly in their native lands as weeds do in our gardens. Others are delicate wildflowers in their natural settings. We shall try to evaluate each plant's needs in the light of its ancestral environment and then put our knowledge to practical use.

We are indebted to horticulturists of the past and present, for it is they who tamed the wildlings and, through a process of selection and hybridization, produced plants which are amenable to house culture. Consider that most common of house plants, the African Violet. Plant breeders have in recent years helped to create such easy-to-grow varieties that untold millions of housewives are able to grow them successfully. Were this not so, the African Violet would be just another wildflower in the back country of Tanganyika.

Every plant discussed in this book may be found in flower shops in the United States and Canada during some month of the year. I have purposely left out some of the less common plants because they cannot be purchased in ordinary trade outlets.

Some of the plants described are easier to grow than others. I shall not gloss over the more difficult ones, but shall try to tell you in a simple and straightforward manner what I believe to be each plant's requirements. Most of the plants mentioned in this book may be easily grown in the average home. After you have learned to accommodate their needs, I hope you will try some of those which require more exacting care. One of the pleasures of horticulture comes with the realization that you have been able to create conditions within your home which satisfy the needs of lovely plants from exotic lands beyond the seas.   J.U.C.

Concord, Massachusetts

WINDOW SILL GARDENING

CHAPTER I

You Are Among Friends

The love of flowers is universal

Years ago I discovered that formal introductions are superfluous when addressing flower lovers. A single comment about the beauty of a flower will swing wide the gate of humble cottage or grand estate. There is a kinship among those who love growing things.

I remember well a tiny farmhouse on the coast of Maine with a trellised porch over which climbed a magnificent purple Clematis, its topmost blossoms lying upon the weathered cedar shingles of the roof. How pleased the dear old lady was when I asked permission to take a picture of her flowers! Then there was the house close beside the road in an upstate Michigan hamlet, where one September day I saw the most beautiful of displays of Autumn Crocus. The proud owner was gratified to know that I cared enough to stop and talk with her about her flowers. Thus are friendships made.

There is a deep yearning for loveliness within the soul of every man, and somehow flowers seem best able to fulfill this inner desire. Consider fire escapes on the walls of crowded tenements. When winter winds whistle through the sheer brick canyons that apartment dwellers know as home, fire escapes stand ready to serve only the one purpose for which they were designed. With the coming of mild weather, though, the picture changes. The first warm day finds rows of plants at every landing, getting a breath of the sparkling air of spring. Then it is that we who admittedly are flower lovers learn how many others share our thirst for beauty.

The odds are with you

One of the most encouraging, yet often overlooked, facts about growing plants is this: the plants with which we work are alive and anxious to do their part—more than that, they often continue to exist when we play the game all wrong. Surely you have seen plants cling tenaciously to life under appalling odds—crammed into undersized pots, forced to subsist on starvation rations or none at all, denied even the regularity of rain from above—and still they live on. If you will learn what plants need for their growth and give them half a chance, they will do the rest!

CHAPTER II

How Plants Grow

Recently I had occasion to talk to a garden group about planting bulbs, and from my point of view the lecture was progressing well when suddenly one of the ladies asked, "What does a Tulip bulb look like?" In a flash I realized that, as far as she was concerned, I had not started at the beginning. To obviate this shortcoming I am including this chapter entitled "How Plants Grow." If some of the material seems elemental to you, then pass over it quickly. These thoughts are directed at beginners, those who do not know and know they do not know.

Light and life

Of the many factors necessary to plant life, such as light, moisture, food, soil, and correct temperatures, none affects house plants more than the amount and quality of light they receive. Light means life. Plants simply cannot carry on their life processes without it, though by our own observations we realize that some plants require more than others.

For a moment, let us consider what we mean when we discuss light as pertaining to plant life. At one end of the scale we have full sunlight and at the other, darkness. A great many of the plants we know out of doors either require or tolerate full sunshine. This need for sunshine is especially true of flowering plants. As we go into the shadows, more space is given over to green plants, whose flowers are fewer and less conspicuous. Ferns are prime examples of plants which enjoy shady places.

House plants, because of the very fact that they have roofs over their heads, must at least be tolerant of some shade. Although we may place our plants at our brightest windows, such locations are no match for the all-around illumination plants enjoy out of doors.

Supplementary light, provided either by incandescent or fluorescent lights, can work wonders with light-starved plants. As you have probably read elsewhere, some commercial growers of African Violets grow their plants entirely by the use of artificial illumination.

In our homes we have what might be called diffused light, such that we can barely see the shadow of our hands when passing them over our plants. Then too, we have areas where it is too dark to cast shadows at all.

It would be well to note here the fact that modern homes are particularly adapted to the growing of house plants. The broad expanses of glass that are an integral part of construction nowadays afford homes many of the light advantages otherwise found only in greenhouses. Perhaps you have noticed how well plants do when they have the advantage of a picture window. It is purely a matter of increased light, the most basic of all requisites to good plant culture.

A sure way of knowing whether your plants are receiving enough light is to check the distance between leaves on vines, for example, or the length of leaf stems on all plants. Excessive length beyond what is normal is an indication that the plants need more light. They are literally *stretching* as they reach toward the light.

Feeding time

The slogan of an English fertilizer manufacturer goes, "Plants don't eat—they drink." With only these five words this company has cut through the mysteries of plant feeding. They have expressed a truth often overlooked even by many good gardeners.

It all goes back to the fact that each plant must assimilate its nourishment dissolved in water. The amounts of food elements in the water, such as nitrogen, phosphorus, potash, iron, boron, manganese, and other trace elements, must be very small, and the basic chemicals must be in a form the plants can use.

With that thought in mind, let us consider the two general types of fertilizers available to us. First, we have the organic fertilizers. Examples of this type are manures, bone meal, cottonseed meal, tankage, or any other fertilizer made directly from animal or plant residue.

To change a material as stubborn, let us say, as bone meal into a basic "soup" that plants can drink not only requires the activity of bacteria in an intermediate stage to reduce the bone meal to its more elemental components, but it also requires time. Organic fertilizers, then, are slow acting, and since only part of them is available at any one time, their effect is long lasting. Also, and very important, it is true that organic fertilizers rarely burn the roots of plants.

The second fertilizer is the inorganic type. The energy for plant growth is in concentrated form and needs only the addition of water to make it available to plants. This factor is both good and dangerous. It is good because we can feed plants and know that the food is ready for their use almost immediately. On the other hand, we are sometimes tempted to be too generous in our application of this kind of fertilizer. When we use too much we produce too lush a growth, or, carrying it to an extreme, we can burn the roots and kill the very plants we intended to help.

When we use inorganic fertilizers we should first read the manufacturer's directions. If he says to use a teaspoonful in a gallon of water, let us not figure that we know better and use a teaspoonful to a quart of water! A little goes a long way. Being water-soluble, inorganic fertilizers quickly wash out of the soil; so we should plan to feed plants more often than if we were using an organic fertilizer.

Generally speaking, the inorganic fertilizers are to be preferred for most house plants because the original soil mixtures, which were prepared by the florist, were well supplied with organic materials, and our only task is to maintain a proper amount of nourishment in the soil. Inorganics, whether liquid, powder, or tablets, are easy to use, odorless, and effective.

Throughout this book you will find references to a complete house-plant fertilizer. This means a fertilizer which contains the three most essential plant-food elements: nitrogen, phosphorus, and potash. There are a great number of fine house-plant fertilizers on the market, some containing traces of additional elements known to be helpful to plant growth. Since fertilizer analyses vary, it is not possible to state correct dosages without consulting the manufacturer's directions for his particular product. For a more comprehensive discussion of fertilizers, refer to the section entitled *Sign language* at the beginning of Chapter XVIII.

Mother earth

Fortunately for beginning gardeners, the plants they buy are already growing in a proper soil, as supplied by their florist, but eventually the time comes when repotting becomes necessary. In this book, under the care of each particular plant, you will find suggested soil mixtures.

All good house-plant soils have certain qualities in common. For one thing, they must have the ability to hold moisture and at the same time be well drained, for no house plant will grow if the soil beneath it stays so soggy that it turns sour. It is also important that the texture of house-plant soils be open enough so that air can get into the soil and friable enough so that the roots can penetrate it easily. It goes without saying that a soil needs to have a balanced supply of nutrients.

A gardener says that a soil is friable when, upon squeezing some of it in his hand, then releasing his fingers, he finds a perfect molded bit of earth, which, at the flick of a finger against the mold, will crumble in his hand. It is a gesture of men of the soil as old as earth's first farmer.

When the heat's on!

One of the nice things about the winter season is that you can concentrate your energies on fewer plants and get more enjoyment from each of them. The hedge does not need trimming, and the lawn is asleep until spring. It is rather pleasant to think that the plants on your window sill are entirely dependent upon your care.

With very few exceptions house plants would like to be cooler than we grow them. Remember then, any plant in flower will stay beautiful longer if it can be kept relatively cool. It is a common practice in our homes to set the thermostat lower at night. This is an excellent idea, for it simulates nature's own design of cool evenings and warm days.

House plants like company

Did you ever notice that the woman who is most successful with house plants usually has something growing on every window sill? We look upon her with envy. We say she has a "green thumb." Then, all too often, we come home and look at the single, sad specimen we have been trying to nurse along and decide that we have no aptitude for growing flowers.

Why not reason a bit as to why her plants do so well? For one thing, we say, her house is more humid than ours, and thus her plants do better. That is one way to look at the picture. If we were to turn it around, we would find that her house is more humid because all of her plants help to make it that way. If you will remember, she waters them every morning, using quarts of fresh water, and by the next day they need water again. That is right; the water she poured into the saucers beneath her plants has been breathed out by the leaves, giving life-sustaining humidity to the room's atmosphere.

MORAL: Grow more plants! If you can keep them fairly close together, you will find that will help, too. Better still, have a plant box at window sill level, and plunge the pots into damp sand, soil, or moss. Moisture from this plant-box area will then be constantly evaporating into the air. By keeping the plants in pots, rather than planting them directly into the soil, you have better control over them. You can replace them or shift them to make more room, and you can turn them occasionally so that their better sides will face into the room.

How to water house plants

We often sum up our errors with a bit of wry philosophy —"Live and learn." The following notes on watering house plants are given in the hope that some of the learning can come without too much bitter experience.

In the first place, we must realize that all plants cannot be treated alike. Plants whose ancestors grew in a warm, moist jungle surely will require more moisture than those of desert origin. We must also recognize the fact that plants lose moisture more or less in proportion to the size of their leaf area. For that reason, we can surmise that a heavy, leafy plant will require more moisture than one with few leaves.

Generally speaking, the following method of watering is satisfactory for most house plants. Pour as much water into the saucers beneath your plants each morning as the plants will absorb by midafternoon. If you have miscalculated and there is still water standing around them at that time of day, pour it off so that the plants will not go to bed with "wet feet." Vary this method occasionally by dipping each pot in a pail of water and giving it a thorough soaking for a few minutes.

You can readily tell when a potted plant is dry by rapping the pot sharply with your knuckles. A dull sound means the plant has enough water; a hollow ring denotes dryness.

Someone is bound to ask at this point, "What do I do if the flowerpot has no drainage hole in the bottom?" This is not such a problem as it seems if one is careful not to overwater. I recommend dipping the pot in a pail of water for a minute or so until most of the air bubbles have stopped rising. Then rest the pot on its side for fifteen or twenty minutes to allow excess moisture to drain away. Do not water again until the soil is fairly dry. In that way the soil will stay aerated and sweet even though the container is glazed and has no drainage hole.

Sometimes new house-plant growers have trouble with plants whose pots have been placed within jardinieres. There is nothing wrong with jardinieres, and they serve a useful purpose in hiding flowerpots, which are not ordinarily decorative. However, it is difficult to judge how much water is in the bottom of a jardiniere, especially if the plant's foliage is thick at the top of the pot. One must be extremely careful not to overwater plants in jardinieres, for unless the water is used by the plants, it will accumulate and rise up on the sides of the pots, excluding oxygen and causing the roots to decay. That is when some folk say, "I can't seem to make plants grow in my house."

Nowadays a great many plants are being grown in plastic pots which have drainage holes in the bottom. I have had exceptional success in growing plants in them and do not hesitate to recommend them highly. You will find that it is not necessary to water plants in plastic pots as frequently as those in clay pots because they do not lose moisture through the sides of the pots.

My final word is on water itself. Although it is not often stressed, I strongly urge that you use warm water on all of your house plants. Cold water cools the soil for hours after its application, which makes it additionally difficult for a plant to thrive under house conditions.

Some researchers say that chlorinated water is not particularly good for house plants, and I suggest that, if your water supply is treated in this manner, you draw off the water for your plants a day in advance and let it sit in an open vessel so that some of the chlorine will escape. As an alternative, use water that has been boiled, for this will have driven off the chlorine also. At a friend's home a short while ago I commented to my hostess about the luxuriance of her African Violets and asked for her secret. She said, "I water them only with rain water." When it rains, she puts a pail under a waterspout and soon has enough water to last her house plants for weeks. Not a bad idea!

Let's have a bath

One of the most beneficial services you can perform for your plants is to keep them clean. Use warm soapy water and a soft cloth to remove dust and grease from both sides of the leaves. Rinse off the soapy water with clear warm water. You will be pleased to see what a regular cleaning program does to get rid of bugs too. They get washed right down the drain. Clean, glossy leaves are not only more beautiful to look at, but naturally they improve a plant's general health. *Do not use any kind of oil on the leaves of your house plants to make them shiny.* Oil clogs the stomata, or breathing pores of the leaves; so they cannot function properly. (See Chapter XV, section entitled *The care of leaves of foliage plants.*)

Do not neglect the fuzzy-leaved plants, such as African Violets, Gloxinias, or Gynuras, either, for they collect dust even more than some of the others. For them I prepare a deep dish of warm soapy water and swish the leaves in it, while holding the plants upside down, being careful, of course, to keep the plants from slipping out of their pots by placing a restraining finger or two on the soil itself. A quick rinse in clear warm water takes the suds away. With African Violets it is essential that you let the foliage dry completely before you put them into a sunny place, or the leaves may be sunburned. Also, I must caution you again, always use water that is warm. Cold water will cause yellow spots to appear on their leaves.

CHAPTER III

African Violets Are Easy

If you already grow African Violets successfully, it is easy for you to agree with the title above. If you still lack the know-how, we hope you will find it in the paragraphs that follow. One thing, at least, should buoy up the spirits of the novice, and that is that millions of people with ordinary homes and average ability grow lovely African Violets. It is not necessary to have a greenhouse or to be a genius.

African Violets at home

We enjoy growing African Violets because they thrive under average house conditions. If your home is comfortable for you, then you can be sure it will suit them also. In the part of Africa where these plants grow wild (Tanganyika), the temperature rarely goes below 50 degrees, or above 100 degrees. Something part way between (in the 70s) is very much to their liking. House temperatures are usually a bit lower at night than during the daytime, which is according to nature's own plan.

The botanical name for African Violets is *Saintpaulia,* derived from the name of their European discoverer Baron Walter von Saint Paul. Perhaps you already realize that African Violets are not true Violets at all. They are members of the family of plants known to botanists as *Gesneria* and are related to Achimenes, Episcia, Isoloma, Streptocarpus, and that wonderful house plant, the Gloxinia.

AFRICAN VIOLETS

AFRICAN VIOLETS

DAFFODIL

TULIPS

GLOXINIAS

CYCLAMENS

TUBEROUS-ROOTED BEGONIAS

GARDENIA

AZALEAS

CARNATIONS

Personal experience

As I write this message to you, I am looking at a row of lovely African Violets on the window sill of my office. They are in full flower, as indeed they have been ever since I purchased them for that spot nearly two years ago. I make this statement to encourage those who say, "Oh, they look beautiful in a flower shop, but I can't grow them at home."

Frankly, these plants of which I speak are far more beautiful now than when I got them. The few things I do for them are easy to do and so free of magic that I hope you will try African Violets yourself and know the pleasure that they can bring with so little effort on your part.

How much light?

My plants sit on a window sill which faces directly north. There are no overhanging trees; so they receive full light, but never any sunshine. Your plants will grow at any window of your house if, in windows that get sun, you make provision to diffuse the strong sun's rays with a protective curtain, or you keep your plants somewhat back from the windows. Plant researchers have found that African Violets do best with light that measures about 1100 foot-candles in intensity. A home rule is this: the light should be just strong enough so that an object held in it will barely cast a shadow on a sunny day.

How often should I water?

Everyone knows that plant roots require water, but there are many who do not realize that air is also essential to the roots of plants. In fact, if the balance between air and water is not correct, the plants will die. Too much air means plants dry out and die; too little air means that oxygen is being excluded, and suffocation results.

One of the nation's foremost growers of African Violets recently pointed out that many home gardeners keep their plants much too wet. Our suggestion for watering is this: set your pots of African Violets in *shallow* saucers into which you place enough *warm* water each morning so that the plants use it up by the middle of the afternoon. Do not let them stand in water all of the time. The roots in the bottom, soggy part of the soil will die if you do.

You will soon find that some plants require more water than others. Treat each plant as the individual that it is, and all of them will do better for you.

Pots

Before I get too far away from the question of moisture, I should like to discuss flowerpots. For many years I have grown African Violets in clay pots and have had very good success with them, but these plants of which I write now are in plastic pots, and they are the happiest I have ever grown. A great number of commercial florists are growing nearly all of their pot plants in plastic pots nowadays.

Cleanup time

Once again I am going to talk about water, but this time from the point of view of cleanliness of your African Violets. As you know, all house plants get dusty, but fuzzy-leaved plants get more than their share. Perhaps you have heard that you cannot let water touch the leaves of your African Violets. How about the rain that falls on them in Africa? The answer is just this: if the water is warmer than room temperature, your plants will be in no danger at all. I wash my plants in a pail of warm sudsy water by tipping them upside down and swishing them around in it until the leaves are thoroughly wet. Then they get a clear rinse of warm water and are allowed to dry in a shady place before going back to the window sill. I always use warm water to prevent yellow spots from developing on the foliage. Perhaps you have seen African Violets with unattractive, blotchy foliage. This unsightly condition is brought about by wetting the leaves with water cooler than room temperature.

Let's eat!

Do African Violets get hungry? Why, surely, just as all plants do. When we consider that all their roots are confined in a cup or two of soil, it is easy to see why additional nutrients are necessary from time to time. However, recent tests have served to convince me of something I have suspected for a long while. That is, African Violets are not heavy feeders, and many persons are being too generous when feeding them. One of the finest African Violet specialists I know says to feed them only one half the strength given in fertilizer directions and, then, only one half as often. So do not kill your plants with kindness. Fertilize with a very mild solution about once a month. If you forget to feed them once in a while, they will not suffer.

Soil preparations

Plants as you get them from your florist do not need to be repotted immediately, but eventually you will want to divide them or shift them to larger pots. I urge that you use one of the prepared "African Violet Soil" mixtures sold at florists and garden supply centers. Not only are these mixtures scientifically correct for your plants, but they are sterilized to kill harmful bacteria, insect pests, and weed seeds. If you want to mix your own soil, use this formula: two parts garden loam, one part leaf mold, one part peat moss or well-rotted manure, and one part sharp sand.

It is well to remember that newly transplanted plants

should not be watered as heavily as established ones and that for the first few days they should be protected from too much light.

Do African Violets rest?

Whether or not African Violets have a definite rest period has been the subject of much controversy over the years. It is my opinion that rest periods are somehow tied in with the genetic background of African Violets. It has been my experience that certain varieties never stop blossoming while others growing beside them seem to have definite periods of resting. There are many intermediate stages too, with some varieties alternating heavy-blossoming periods with times when they produce only a few flowers.

Practically speaking, I believe in treating African Violets as though they do not have a resting period. I try at all times to provide optimum growth conditions, since plants will blossom only when they are in active growth. Over the years there has been a tremendous improvement in the everblooming qualities of African Violets. Those varieties which prove to be shy bloomers fall by the wayside, and the more productive ones take their places.

Sick plants

At the risk of seeming hardhearted, I am going to stress my firm belief concerning sick house plants. *Take them, pots and all, to the nearest trash barrel, and dispose of them.* A sick plant will infect your healthy ones. Even after you have removed the cause of a plant's illness, it takes months of convalescence before it looks well again. A window sill is not a hospital!

The best cure is really a preventive. Start with healthy plants and quarantine all new plants you acquire for a few weeks before placing them with your healthy ones. The old adage that says, "An ounce of prevention is worth a pound of cure" was never more appropriate than when applied to plants.

If you wash your plants regularly, as we have suggested, you will probably wash away any insects that might be on the plants. The lone exception is the Cyclamen mite. This little creature works deep down in the crowns of the plants and causes the leaves to curl and twist and to become very hairy. Still worse, the plants refuse to blossom. Here is a prime example of what I mean when I say to throw the bugs away, along with the plant!

If you must play doctor, try capsules of sodium selanate according to directions on the package, or use a new material called Kelthane EC (two teaspoonfuls per gallon of water). Make two applications, a week apart, and be sure to wet the crowns of the plants thoroughly.

New plants from old

About the easiest job in the world is to start a new African Violet plant from the leaf of an old one. Use a leaf that is neither old nor young; choose a mature leaf that is free of insects or disease. Stick the stem of it in water or sand, and in a few weeks it will develop roots and a new crown of leaves as well. Pot the new plant in prepared African Violet Soil, and in a few months you will have another flowering plant for your window sill.

CHAPTER IV

Cyclamens — Love at First Sight

If someone should tell you that you could have a beautiful flowering plant, but in order to see its first flower you would have to take care of the plant for five hundred days and nights, no one would think you queer if you suggested that the return would not warrant the investment of your time. Fortunately for us, the men who grow Cyclamens for a livelihood have great patience. Starting with seeds, Cyclamen growers give their plants constant attention for a year and a half before they are ready for market. Think of how many times they have been nourished, transplanted, protected from heat, cold, and insects, and of the countless occasions they have had to be watered.

Getting acquainted

If you have never met a Cyclamen, ask for an introduction the next time you visit your florist, and be prepared for love at first sight. If Cyclamens are in season (autumn, winter, or early spring), you have a real thrill in store. Not only will you be excited by the exotic, swept-back petals of each flower, that make the blossoms look like a flock of delicate birds poised for flight, but if you will pull aside the foliage and peer into the crowns of the plants, you will find scores of buds at all stages of development, promising still greater beauty in the weeks ahead.

It is not fair to describe the colors of Cyclamen blossoms in such prosaic terms as red or pink because there are so many subtle variations in shading from plant to plant. The largest color grouping is among the rosy shades, ranging from the palest blush through all the lovely gradations to deep red. Some others have a lavender touch, and plants may be found whose flowers are of the most delicate lilac, or at the other end of the scale, nearly purple. Beyond all these are the white Cyclamens, surely among the most exquisite of all white flowers. As an added distinction, some plants bear flowers whose petals are intricately frilled along the edges, and there are even double-flowering forms to be found occasionally. All Cyclamens bear their flowers in great abundance, held high above their dark foliage, itself often marked by glistening zones of silvery white.

Moisture and sunshine

In my home I grow Cyclamens from October until late March on a wide window sill facing south. The pots sit in trays filled with moist pebbles. Each day they are watered from the tops of the pots with enough water so that the moisture level in the trays actually rises about one fourth of an inch up on the sides of the pots. By midafternoon the moisture level falls to the pebble level, but the soil in the pots stays constantly moist.

During the time of the year we consider Cyclamens as house plants (midautumn until early spring), it is well to give them as much sunlight as you can. When grown through the summer months, they need partial shade, but winter sun is mild enough so that its direct rays are beneficial to the plants.

Keep them cool

Cyclamens simply must have a cool place in order to do well. In a greenhouse they are grown at a night temperature of 50 degrees to 55 degrees and as close to that as possible during the daylight hours. Such a climate is a bit too chilly for most of us, but, even so, a place can probably be found in a cool room close to a window (where it is cooler still), where a Cyclamen will do well. The Cyclamens in my home do well in a room where the thermostat is set at 65 degrees at night. Being close to a window, the plants are somewhat cooler than that. One good friend of mine is so captivated by Cyclamens that she grows her plants on the window sill of a cool bedroom and brings them into the living room only on "state" occasions!

It is a good idea to feed Cyclamens every two weeks during their flowering season to keep the flowers up to size and the plants healthy. Use a very mild solution of a complete house-plant fertilizer. As with all house plants, it is better not to feed them at all than to give them too much.

Cyclamens grow from beetlike corms, which are planted so that the top third of each corm is above the level of the soil. All of a plant's leaves and flowers spring from the surface of its bulbous root. Whenever a leaf turns yellow or a flower fades, take its stem in your hand, and give it a sharp twisting tug. It will disengage itself from the corm without any damage to the plant.

Your Cyclamens next year

It is quite possible to keep Cyclamens over for several years. Here is one way to do it. After flowers fade, continue to feed and water your plants as though they were still blossoming, and when the weather becomes mild, plunge them, pot and all, outdoors in a lightly shaded section of your garden, where you will remember to water them often during hot weather. (See chapter on "Summer Care of House Plants" for plunging directions.)

It may be that your Cyclamens need to be repotted, and if that is true, a good time to do the job is just before the plants go outside for the summer. Use a soil made up of two parts leaf mold, one part sand, and one part loam. If these ingredients are not available, we suggest that you use the potting mixture sold for African Violets, and to it add about one fourth sand. This soil is usually packed in plastic bags so that it stays moist, and since it is sterilized, it is free of weed seeds and diseases. You can buy it in small quantities from your florist or garden center. As to the actual operation of repotting your Cyclamens, simply shake off the old soil and plant the corms firmly in the new soil in such a way that the top third of each corm is above the soil level in the pot.

Cyclamen mites

The pest most likely to bother your Cyclamens is known as the Cyclamen mite. This insect works deep down in the crowns of such plants as Cyclamens and African Violets and is the chief reason that some people cannot make their plants blossom. The material Kelthane EC, mentioned under the care of African Violets, is the latest insecticide available to kill Cyclamen mites. Use two teaspoonfuls of Kelthane EC in a gallon of water. Make two sprayings, a week apart. Unless the directions on an insecticide package specifically say it will kill Cyclamen mites, it probably will not kill them.

Back to nature

It may interest you to know that there are many kinds of Cyclamens growing as wildflowers in parts of Europe and Asia Minor. Some of the hardy species make delightful rock-garden plants for outdoor plantings. The ancestors of our florist type of Cyclamen are supposed to have come from the island of Cyprus about two hundred years ago. They are not hardy outdoors.

The old English writers referred to a type of wild Cyclamen as "Sowbread" because it was a favorite food of foraging swine. Another odd fact to remember about Cyclamens is that they belong to the Primrose family, although they seem to the untrained eye to be so unlike Primroses. In Switzerland children gather bunches of a wild Cyclamen, which they call *Alpenveilchen* (Alpine Violet).

CHAPTER V

Poinsettias

Mexican wildflowers

As surely as a bluebird is a sign of spring, a Poinsettia is a token of the Christmas season. Yet this was not always true. Although we think of Poinsettias as Christmas flowers, they were not growing in Bethlehem at the time of Christ's birth. Poinsettias came to the attention of the horticultural world little more than a century ago when the United States Minister to Mexico, Dr. Joel R. Poinsett, sent plants of this scarlet wildflower home to a friend in Philadelphia. Today Poinsettias are dooryard flowers throughout the tropical and subtropical lands of the world, as well as the most popular of all house plants at the Christmas season.

It is easy to get the idea that it was a simple step from Mexican wildflower to world-wide house plant, but such a notion would be misleading. In nature Poinsettias often grow to be twelve feet tall in ragged clumps that defy house culture, to say the least. It took many years of selection and plant breeding to produce the large-flowered forms we enjoy today. Over the years men have chosen specimens whose flowers were especially colorful, whose foliage was particularly green and attractive, whose manner of growth and response to pot culture was outstanding, and from these have evolved the Poinsettias we know today.

Care as house plants

It is fortunate for us that Poinsettias are by nature accustomed to the semitropical temperatures of our homes.

Most specialists agree that they do best at about 65 degrees. If your home is kept at 70 degrees, your Poinsettias should still be happy. In fact, I am convinced that Poinsettias are far more apt to be injured by a cold draft or chilling in transit than by being in a room where the temperature is slightly above the ideal.

In the same breath with temperature must be mentioned humidity, for they go together to determine whether or not any house plant will be happy. In modern homes a humid atmosphere is difficult to achieve. Perhaps the best we can do is to grow plants in trays filled with moist pebbles so that moisture evaporating around the plants will be of benefit to them. Even this amount of humidity does help them grow well, though it cannot approach the highly humid conditions prevailing in our grandmothers' kitchens.

We must remember that plants with leaves as large and thin as those of Poinsettias require a great deal of moisture every day. The soil beneath your plants should always be moist, but not soggy. As a practical matter, put saucers or trays beneath your plants and see that they have enough *warm* water in them each morning so that the plants use it up by the middle of the afternoon. Do not let them go to bed with "wet feet."

Here is another side to the moisture story: if a Poinsettia lacks moisture it begins to retrench immediately. Right away it seems to decide that it should sacrifice some of its lower leaves; so overnight they turn yellow and fall off. Let us say that at this point the plant begins to receive sufficient moisture. It will try once again to lead a normal life, but another short drought, and all the plant will have left is a few red tail feathers on some gawky stalks!

Poinsettias will not do well for even a short period of time unless you give them an abundance of light. They should be close to a window if you expect to grow them happily for more than a few days. Direct sun is not necessary all day long, but surely a few hours of morning or afternoon sun should be considered essential. Whenever I think about the light requirements of Poinsettias I am reminded of a store window in my town that starts off the holiday season each year with a pair of Poinsettias. In March these flowers are still in bloom as happily as though they had never left the greenhouse. The moral is this: that big store window faces *south*.

The toll of time

Sooner or later you must face up to a fact of life regarding your Poinsettia. The reason you bought it in the first place was that the flowers were pretty. More than that, from the point of view of the plant the flowers were an indication that it was approaching maturity—and the next step in a Poinsettia's life cycle is a period of complete rest! It is hoped that the cultural suggestions which precede this paragraph will enable you to put off this rest period as long as possible. With good care a Christmas Poinsettia should still be pretty during the latter part of January. There are many flower lovers who keep their plants a month longer than that; so you have every reason to give yours good care.

After your Poinsettia has dropped its leaves and is no longer attractive, you have a decision to make. Are you going to throw the plant away, or are you going to try to grow it on for another year? Let us face it—the man who grew your Poinsettia in the first place was a specialist, and he was around at the right time with water each day, and shading, fertilizer, repotting, staking, and insect control in season. We cannot hope as amateurs to succeed as well as he, no matter how careful we are. Frankly, I suggest that

you throw away your Poinsettia after it has lost the bloom
of youth!

Doing it yourself

As surely as I feel worn-out Poinsettias should be con-
signed to their final resting places, I know that there are
those who will want to try their hand at carrying a Poinsettia over to another Christmas. For their guidance I have
some concrete suggestions, which will work if followed
carefully. When a Poinsettia has dropped its foliage and is
no longer ornamental, stop watering it and put the plant
in a cool place (above freezing) until spring. In April or
May cut the plant down to within four inches of the pot
and plunge the pot in a pail of water for a few minutes
to give it a good drink. From that point forward, apply
just enough water to keep the soil barely moist until new
growth starts; then water as for any growing plant.

It is a good idea to give your Poinsettia a bit of fertilizer
as soon as new growth is apparent. The object of this initial
fertilizer is to build the plant up to a point where you can
get some sturdy cuttings from it later in the summer. Use
a complete house-plant fertilizer every two weeks to keep
the plant growing robustly. As soon as weather is warm,
plunge the plant, pot and all, in a sheltered spot out of
doors where it will get sunshine but not be whipped by
drying winds. (See chapter on "Summer Care of House
Plants" for plunging instructions.)

In August and September take cuttings of sturdy top
growth of your plants about four to six inches long and
root them in sand. They will root more easily if the cut
stem is dusted with a rooting powder. When new roots are
formed pot the young plants in individual pots and grow
them in the house. As a potting mixture we suggest one
made up of two parts loam, one part well-rotted manure,

and one part sand. This is not a rich potting soil, but is what Poinsettias like at this stage in their growth. As they take hold and begin to grow, fertilize every two weeks with a complete house-plant fertilizer in mild solution. When you are sure you have a crop of young plants started throw away the old plant.

Plants grown as we have suggested above should be in flower at Christmas time. There is one additional factor which must be considered, however, when you try to grow Poinsettias in the house throughout the year. Poinsettias are what botanists call "short-day" plants: they will blossom only during the short days of the year. If you grow your Poinsettias in a room where they receive artificial light on autumn evenings, they will not blossom but will continue to grow only green leaves, because artificial light during the evenings will give the plants the equivalent of a summer's day of sunlight. You must find a way to shade home-grown Poinsettias from additional light from sunset until dawn. Moving them into a closet may be the answer, but if it is, it is another reason why most flower lovers let the professionals grow Poinsettias!

Flowers that are not flowers

One last note about Poinsettias: it is true that the parts of the plants we call flowers are not the real flowers. They are colorful bracts or, more simply, modified leaves. The true flowers are the nectar-covered chartreuse nubs found in the centers of the bracts. Poinsettia bracts may be any one of several shades of red, as well as pink or white. There is even a double-flowered form which does well out of doors in the South, but it is not a satisfactory pot plant.

CHAPTER VI

Gardenias Are for Memories

Nostalgia

Gardenias—Southern girls call them Cape Jasmines, but their fragrance is the same, that haunting sweetness which brings back memories of first corsages and junior proms. Is there a housewife who has not wanted to grow a Gardenia plant of her own in her own home? We wish we could say that they are easy to grow, but we cannot. Yet there are thousands of women who grow them without apparent effort.

It can be done!

Not long ago I visited a friend's home, and there on a table beside a picture window was a lovely Gardenia plant, covered with buds in all stages of development. My hostess said that last year her plant had sixteen flowers open all at the same time, and, from appearances, this year's crop of buds will do even better. So—it can be done! Gardenias can be grown in your home, but I must warn you that they do require a bit of special attention.

Meet their needs

Gardenia plants need as much sunshine as you can possibly give them throughout the year. Choose a spot for them with that in mind, for without ample light your Gardenias surely will not blossom.

The next "must" for Gardenias is moist soil. Gardenias enjoy soil much wetter than would be tolerated by most other plants. Specialists growing them never let the soil beneath their plants become dry; so we should take their lesson to heart.

The third essential for happy Gardenias is to grow them in acid soil. If you have occasion to repot yours, use a mixture of one half soil and one half peat moss. The peat moss will give your plants an acid soil to begin their growth, but you must maintain the acidity to keep their leaves a rich, glossy green. Water your plants once a month with a solution made of one ounce of iron sulphate in two gallons of water. (Iron sulphate costs only pennies from your druggist.)

In order to produce flowers a Gardenia plant has to be in active growth. This condition can be encouraged by providing a regular source of food and by maintaining correct temperatures. Professional Gardenia growers feed their plants every three or four weeks with a solution made of one ounce of ammonium sulphate to two gallons of water. For home culture we suggest you give your plants a monthly feeding of a mild solution of a complete houseplant fertilizer.

Gardenia plants set their flower buds when night temperatures are between 60 degrees and 65 degrees. Day temperatures are relatively unimportant as long as they are higher than those at night.

Gardenias in the summertime

Gardenias seem to benefit to a remarkable degree by having a summer vacation outdoors. Give them a spot where they can have an abundance of light but some protection from the sun at midday. Since flower-bud formation occurs when temperatures are about 60 degrees, you will find relatively few flowers on your plants in midsummer because it is too warm. As the temperature drops on autumn evenings, however, buds will be initiated which will continue to develop into flowers when the plants are brought back into the house. Make the transition from garden to house before there is any danger of frost.

Special problems

Would-be Gardenia growers are apt to meet with two common difficulties, both of which can be overcome rather easily. The first is that the leaves may turn yellowish in color. Usually this is caused by the soil's becoming too alkaline. Use the solution of iron sulphate as mentioned above. If this does not turn the leaves green in a month or so, throw the plants away because they are probably infested with root nematodes or have stem canker, both of which are practically incurable.

The second cause for alarm is known as "bud drop." It is rather disconcerting to grow a Gardenia right up to the point at which the buds seem about to open, only to have them drop off the plant with a deathly finality. Several factors can cause bud drop, but if your plants are apparently healthy, bud drop is probably the result of lack of sunshine or insufficient water in the soil or in the air. Greenhouse growers syringe their plants with water regularly to raise the humidity of the air around them. You may find it helpful to wet the foliage of your plants, too, especially when the air is excessively hot and dry.

Gardenias are not easy to grow as house plants, but it can be done! The joy you will experience with the opening of each new flower makes it worth all the extra effort necessary to please their finicky natures.

CHAPTER VII

Spring—Flowering Bulbs

TULIPS—HYACINTHS—DAFFODILS—PAPER-WHITE NARCISSUS

Four hundred years of Tulips

In 1554 Augier Ghislain de Busbecq was the Austrian ambassador to the court of the Sultan of Turkey. It was he who first sent seeds of Tulips to Vienna in that year. Thus began one of the most singular tales in the annals of horticulture. Five years later Tulips were in flower in Austria. Seeds from these plants, as well as new importations from Turkey, were soon being grown throughout Europe.

Holland entered the picture at an early date, for its soil and climate were peculiarly suited to their culture. By 1600 Tulip growing had become a national pastime for the Dutch, each grower striving to produce newer and better varieties than his neighbor. All went well until 1634, when the desire for new varieties among the trade-wealthy merchants led them to pay enormous prices (as much as 13,000 florins, about $3500 in today's exchange) for a single bulb. After four years of this "tulipomania" prices receded to normal levels.

Today, as never before, Tulips are linked in our minds with the Netherlands. Each year Holland ships to the United States alone over five hundred million bulbs, the majority of which are Tulips. Lest we in this country get the idea that we buy all of Holland's bulbs, it is well to remember that on a per-capita basis England buys three bulbs to our one, and Sweden nearly ten times as many bulbs per person!

Sometimes we get the idea that all bulbs are grown in

Holland, but this is not true. Some of the finest Daffodils in the world, as well as most of the Easter Lily bulbs used in this country, are grown in the Pacific Northwest. Tulip bulbs are being grown commercially in Michigan with outstanding success.

Buried treasure

Perhaps you cannot remember when you first learned that Tulips, Hyacinths, and Narcissus grow from bulbs. Yet to begin our discussion, this very fact must be made clear for the benefit of newcomers to the guild of gardeners.

Bulbs might be described as "condensed plants," for in a real sense that is what they are. During periods of dormancy bulbous plants withdraw themselves into hard, fat balls of living tissue and emerge again only when conditions are favorable to their growth.

Normally, the plants we know as Dutch bulbs spend up to three fourths of every year hidden from our sight. Their bulbous roots store food throughout the dry summer and the cold winter. Leaves and flowers rise and fade in the three brief months of springtime.

The real lesson we must learn from the information above is this: if we intend to keep our bulbs growing and nourished so that they will be satisfactory for another season, we must care for them properly during this short interval each year when they are in active growth. Most of the good we can do for pot-grown bulbs must be done in the period from the time the flowers fade until the plants go into their rest period.

All flower lovers hate to throw away living plants. If we realize that beneath every Hyacinth blossom, for example, there is a bit of "buried treasure," that there is a "coupon in every package," we shall have the initiative to save the bulbs and enjoy them in our gardens for years to come.

Blossomtime

There is very little to do for pots of spring-flowering bulbs when they are in blossom except to enjoy them! It is true that they will need a big drink of water each day and that the cooler they can be grown, the longer they will last. Most of us find the cool, damp days of early spring too chilly for shirt-sleeve comfort, yet it is this climate which pleases spring-flowering bulbs most of all. Be sensible with your bulbous plants: give them as cool a place in the house as you can, keep the soil beneath them quite moist, and be sure that they have an abundance of sunlight.

Protecting your investment

As soon as the flowers fade, remove the pots of bulbs to a less conspicuous location, but one in which they can be cool and moist and can have the benefit of sunshine. Feed them with a complete house-plant fertilizer as soon as they finish flowering and again in one week. Then simply let them grow as long as they will. Eventually the leaves will turn yellow and wither away. Stop watering and let the soil get completely dry.

You may store the bulbs in the dry soil of the pots until autumn planting season, you may take the bulbs out of the pots and keep them over summer in a dry place out of the sun, or you may simply plant them in your garden right away. In any case, enrich the soil with a liberal dusting of bone meal, and plant the bulbs three times as deep as their longest diameter. There is no reason that bulbs treated in this manner will not flower in your garden for years to come, though they will not do well as potted plants again. Tulips and Hyacinths may eventually fade away, but members of the Narcissus family will multiply and become more beautiful with each passing year.

Dunce cap

Modern children do not know what dunce caps are, but ask some of the older folk! The caps we have in mind, however, are to encourage the "higher education" of Hyacinths, not children!

No other bulb will give more satisfaction than a well-grown Hyacinth. Not only are the flowers lovely, but their fragrance seems to conjure up thoughts of springtime. It is easy to grow Hyacinths in special Hyacinth glasses, which are broad-based flasks with narrow necks and flaring tops made to fit the bases of Hyacinth bulbs. They are a real joy to grow, since you may watch not only the leaves and flowers but also the action of the roots through the clear glass.

Start with the largest-sized bulbs you can buy. Fill your Hyacinth glasses up to their necks with fresh water, and set the bulbs into the cuplike tops. The water must almost, but not quite, touch the bottoms of the bulbs. Set them in a cool, dark location.

Within days white whiskers of roots will descend from the bottoms of the bulbs down into the water. It is at this point that the "dunce caps" come into play. You see, Hyacinths have a habit of flowering before the stems have elongated enough to grow out of the bulbs. This results in malformed plants and unsatisfactory flowers. By placing opaque cones, or dunce caps, over each bulb, you can make the stems stretch out as they would normally out of doors. When they are about three inches tall remove the cones, bring the plants into a light place, and within days your room will be filled with the entrancing fragrance of springtime!

A *host of Daffodils*

Whether you call them Daffodils, Narcissus, or Jonquils has no influence upon their vernal loveliness. Suffice it to say that botanically they are members of the Narcissus family, no matter what other designation they may be given.

When you plant your Narcissus out of doors, do so early in the fall. September seems to be the best month of the year to plant them. Whether your bulbs are some you have saved from pots of spring flowers, or whether they are newly purchased bulbs, plant them deep enough. I suggest four to six inches of soil, *measured, not guessed at,* above the top of each bulb. In heavy soil four inches is enough; in lighter land they will do better when planted six inches deep.

Remember that flowers are a crop just as are the vegetables in your garden; so prepare the soil as faithfully as you would for an edible crop. For fertilizer use enough bone meal so as to whiten the top of the soil; then fork it into the soil thoroughly.

Narcissus are especially lovely when planted in informal groups, or "drifts" as they are sometimes called. Scatter them under the branches of a tree or along the edges of a lawn; cluster them at the foot of a boulder or under the shelter of a wall. In any case, plant them where they fall, just as you have scattered them. If you don't, your inborn sense of geometry will exert itself, and your flowers will come up in rows like forlorn little soldiers!

Canary Islander

Almost everyone can recognize a Paper-white Narcissus, but how many would guess that its cousins grow wild among the volcanic rocks of the Canary Islands? Botanists tell us that there are over one hundred distinct varieties of this flower to be found in various parts of the world, some as far away as China and Japan.

I want to discuss Paper-whites because they are plants which the youngest and most inexperienced flower lover can grow, yet which never fail to awaken our sense of beauty, though we have grown them for decades. Perhaps even more important, they may be grown easily by those whose gardening activities are limited to a single window sill.

Over the years all of us have heard folk say that their plants grow too tall or sometimes that the buds fail to open. Since each bulb has its flower already formed within its onionlike body when we buy it, what we need to know is the correct method of encouraging it to open to its fullest fragrant beauty.

A plant without roots is a sad spectacle indeed; so our first interest in these rootless bulbs is to grow a "full beard" on the base of each of them. Roots grow best in darkness; so the bulbs must spend the first few weeks after planting in a cool, dark location. First, however, plant your bulbs in shallow dishes, using pearl chips, sand, or fiber to hold them erect. Set them so that the top half of each bulb shows above the planting medium, and put enough water in each bowl so that the bottom third of each bulb is sitting in water. Now they should go to the cool, dark spot you have chosen, where they should stay until top growth is two or three inches tall. You must add water to them regularly during this period, or the roots will dry up and perish.

By the time the top growth is established, the bowls are full of clean, white roots, and it is time to move the plants to a bright, cool window sill. From this point on they are things of beauty, for each day you can watch the gradual unfolding of their leaves and the appearance of the bud sheaths. Their loveliness is apparent long before their flowers open.

During this period two factors will determine the ultimate quality of the flowers. They are an abundance of light and cool temperatures. In a dimly lighted spot or under warm conditions top growth shoots up very fast, but without the firm texture we desire. Grow your bulbs in the coolest spot you can that is above freezing, and keep them in a place where the sun can reach them.

One last thought: plant a dish of Paper-whites, or the yellow variety, Soleil d'Or, every week from September until Christmas, and you will have a constant supply of flowers. Do not plant the white and yellow varieties together, since they do not mature at the same time. Also, throw away the bulbs after flowering; they are not worth saving.

Bargain bulbs

The next two paragraphs can do more to ensure your success with bulbs than all the others which have preceded them. Please do not be taken in by the glamorous advertisements which offer "a garden full of bulbs for $1" or words to that effect. See your florist for your bulbs. He sells quality, and without that one ingredient all your other efforts will have been in vain. If a florist could produce good flowers from cheap bulbs he would do so, but he knows that it cannot be done.

As an example of what I mean, consider that florists often pay several times as much for their own bulbs at wholesale as the price at which the bargain bulbs are offered at retail! If you are going to spend a dollar on bulbs, get a dozen top-size bulbs, not one hundred runts. *The only bargain in bulbs is quality!*

CHAPTER VIII

Caladiums — Living Rainbows

Imagine for yourself plants whose leaves are shaped like spearheads sized for a Goliath, clothe them in the colors of Joseph's coat, and see them, in your mind's eye, growing on the floor of the rain forests of Brazil and Peru. Here are Caladiums, living rainbows! We have heard children call them "Elephant Ears," and the direct approach of youth perhaps comes closest of all to describing them in a few words.

Caladiums are flowering plants whose insignificant flowers are rarely noticed. Try to find them for yourself someday. They look like discouraged Calla Lilies, never attaining enough beauty to rival the multicolored leaves among which they nestle. Caladium leaves may be pink, red, white, or green, in solid colors or mottled patterns, often with dark veins outlined against the more transparent sections of the foliage.

Caladiums in the summertime

Caladiums might well be called summer house plants, for they are usually started into growth by florists in March and by mid-October lose their foliage and rest completely until spring. The time in which they are in active growth includes the hot summer months, when few other pot plants are available. The rhizomes from which Caladiums grow are planted in greenhouse flats in a soil mixture which is mostly peat moss. They are given warm, humid conditions with temperatures ranging from 75 degrees to 80 degrees, much like those that exist in the jungles from which their ancestors came. After new roots have appeared the young plants are potted separately into a somewhat lighter soil and allowed to grow larger for retail sales.

You will find few house plants of any season more beautiful than well-grown Caladiums. Perhaps more important than any other thing to some flower lovers is the fact that these lovely plants do not need a sunny location in which to grow well. Their leaves are very thin and delicate, and you will find that they do best of all in a spot just out of the sun, where there is an abundance of light, but no possibility of burning. A similar situation would suit other lovely plants such as Gloxinias, African Violets, and Tuberous-rooted Begonias, one or more of which you might like to grow in company with Caladiums for the variety they can give your summer window sill.

Using Caladiums outdoors

Caladiums are not grown out of doors as much as they should be. This is true because many gardeners are unaware of their potentialities as garden plants. For example, one of the most beautiful window boxes I have ever seen was on a house in a small Pennsylvania town under the shade of big Maple trees. Such a location would discourage most plants, but the Caladiums there were at their best, lending their brilliant colors to brighten the shadows.

Food and drink

Caladiums need to be fed regularly. Every two weeks during their growing season you should enrich one of their drinks with a complete house-plant fertilizer. The soil in which they are growing when you buy them is ordinarily one half loam and one half peat moss. If you have occasion to repot your Caladiums and cannot get this material, use a prepared African Violet Soil. Its mixture, high in organic matter, is ideal for Caladiums.

While we are concerning ourselves with the soil for Caladiums we should consider moisture also. Although they are watered sparingly when they are first started into growth in the spring, it is essential that the soil stay quite moist during their growing season. It is only when Caladiums start to rest that water is gradually withheld from them.

Sleeping beauties

About six to eight months after your Caladium was started into growth it will begin its rest period. No amount of water or coaxing will keep it growing any longer; so you might as well face the fact that it needs rest. When you notice more and more of the leaves losing their beauty water less frequently, and when they wither entirely store the plant, pot and all, in a dry place at about 50 degrees to 60 degrees until the following spring. Repot then in the soil we have suggested, and your plant will grow bigger and prettier another year.

Fish and poi

No story about Caladiums would be complete without mention of their famous cousin the Taro plant. Ground Taro root is the chief ingredient of poi, so much a part of Hawaiian feasts. Some botanists claim that Taro, a mainstay in the diet of Pacific island people since the dawn of history, is a *Caladium*. Others, drawing a finer line, call Taro *Colocasia*, but to any man their kinship is readily apparent.

Their leaves are typical "elephant ears," and they grow in swampy areas as do Caladiums, showing by their affinity to moisture another tie to their more brilliantly colored relatives from Latin America.

CHAPTER IX

Azaleas in the Home

In England there is an Azalea, growing in a flowerpot, known to be over a hundred and fifty years old! It has been in its present flowerpot for more than fifty years! In Japan, where pot culture of nearly every kind of plant is an ancient art, there are Azaleas which have been grown for centuries in flowerpots, being passed down as precious heirlooms from generation to generation. I mention these indisputable facts for two reasons: first, to question those who would throw away an Azalea simply because its present crop of flowers has faded and, second, to encourage those who would like to grow these wonderful pot plants in their own homes. It is my opinion that no other florist plants can give more satisfaction than Azaleas. They are amazingly free flowering. If you will examine an Azalea plant closely, you will find that the tip of nearly every branch ends in a cluster of buds or blossoms. How can you possibly improve on a situation like that?

Types of florist Azaleas

While it is true that almost any kind of an Azalea can be grown in a flowerpot, this discussion will be limited to the three main groups of evergreen Azaleas grown as pot plants. The large-flowered varieties, usually grown on single stems like little trees, are grouped botanically under the heading of *Azalea indica*. Many of their flowers are double or semidouble in form, and individual blossoms are often two or three inches in diameter. I have many times heard flower buyers ask for "that beautiful Rosebush," while pointing at an Indica Azalea; perhaps that describes it best of all. In color they may be pure white, pink, pink and white, or a shade of crimson purple or crimson red.

You will never forget your first meeting with the second type of Azaleas we shall consider. As a group they are known as Kurume Azaleas, but the name gives little hint of their loveliness. Kurumes have literally hundreds, and sometimes thousands, of flowers on a single plant, depending upon its size. The flowers are often so close together that there is no indication that the plants have any leaves at all! Kurumes may be snowy white, any shade of pink from the most delicate blush to "watermelon" pink; they may be brick red, purplish red, cerise, or salmon. In any case, their flowers are a sight to gladden the heart of any lover of beauty.

Plant breeders have in recent years brought into being a third group of Azaleas known as Rutherfordianas. They have produced a whole series of new hybrids, using both Indicas and Kurumes as parents, and, in addition, have introduced bloodlines from other Azalea species. The result is a wealth of new plants, many with subtle colors never before seen in florist Azaleas. Some plants favor one parent, and some the other, but in general the flower size is somewhere between Indicas and Kurumes, with the free-flowering habit of the Kurume parent very much in evidence.

Azalea cousins

When grown as house plants, all florist-type Azaleas require the same environment. In order that you may understand their needs more completely, we shall begin with a résumé of their place in the plant world. Botanists group them among the *Ericaceae;* so they are members of the same family of plants as Rhododendron, Mountain Laurel,

Heather, Blueberry, Andromeda, Leucothoë, and Rhodora. Even the Mayflower of New England, *Epigaea repens*, known also as Trailing Arbutus, is a member of the same family as Azaleas.

All of these plants have one particular thing in common besides their botanical likenesses, and that is their need for acid soil. All of them revel in acid peat moss, and, in fact, for the home gardener I can suggest no soil mixture for Azaleas which will suit them better than peat moss, alone or with a bit of sand added to it.

The blossoming season of Azaleas when considered as house plants starts about Christmas time each year and extends into April, although no one plant blossoms for that entire period. It is normal for Kurume Azalea flowers to stay beautiful for two weeks, or even longer, if conditions approach the ideal. The Indica Azaleas, because all of their flowers do not open at once, are often lovely for a month.

Azaleas on your winter window sill

When grown outdoors, Azaleas are spring-flowering shrubs; so if we want to please them indoors, we must try to duplicate springtime conditions in our homes. The only difficulty is that spring is often cold and is usually damp, quite the opposite of the conditions prevailing in most homes!

In order to simulate spring, we should move Azaleas as close to our windows as possible, where coolness coming through the glass will give them a touch of the weather they desire. A temperature of 60 degrees to 65 degrees in the daytime and 50 degrees to 55 degrees at night will suit them very well. If your rooms are warmer, then accept the fact that the flowers will not last as long as they would if you could grow them at cooler temperatures. Your Azaleas will stay beautiful longest of all if you can set the plants in a cooler place during the night. Even a few degrees will help them appreciably, though, of course, they must not be subjected to freezing temperatures.

Azaleas must be constantly moist. If they are allowed to dry out severely just once, they are apt to drop all their leaves or even die. I urge that you not only water your plants often enough from the tops of the pots to keep the soil moist, but that you set the pots on trays of sand or pebbles that are kept moist at all times. Evaporation from the trays helps to give an extra amount of humidity in the immediate area of the plants.

Along with their need for water there is a similiar need for light. All through the winter months Azaleas will do well on your brightest window sill. It is only during the hotter months of the year that they need shade from the direct rays of the sun. An east window is an ideal place for an Azalea in the wintertime, since there it can get the benefit of early morning sun, plus an abundance of light during the balance of the hours of daylight.

Care after flowering

Shortly after flowers fade, and sometimes earlier, Azaleas begin their vegetative growth in preparation for next year's flowers. At the base of each flower cluster, several new shoots sprout forth, and in a matter of a week or so the plants transform themselves from lovely flowering plants to beautiful foliage plants. The care of your Azaleas at this stage in their growth will determine to a great degree the success or failure you will experience with them throughout the rest of the year. It is now that the plants need food, and a feeding with a complete house-plant fertilizer, according to manufacturer's directions, is in order. About two weeks later feed your plants once more. Under normal conditions this will be enough plant food for the year. It is true that commercial growers feed more often, but house plants should not be encouraged to grow out of bounds.

Out they go!

Before I write about the summer care of Azaleas out of doors, I feel that I should preface my remarks with a statement that I realize that many of my readers live in sections where Kurumes and even the tenderer Indicas are grown as garden shrubs. The observations I am about to make are intended for those who wish to grow their Azaleas as pot plants throughout the year or who live in cooler regions, where these Azaleas cannot survive winter weather out of doors.

Now that the weather differential has been taken into account, let us return to the Azaleas on your window sill. As soon as all danger of frost is over, your plants should be moved outside. Leave them in their pots, but bury the pots up to their rims in peat moss or sand, preferably the former. Do so in a location which will afford the plants protection from the sun during the hot part of the day. Azalea growers usually put their plants under lath shade until the first week of August. Then the shade is removed so that the growth will harden before cold weather. For the first few days after the shading is removed, they are watered often to be sure their tender growth does not dry out.

This brings us to the most important part of summer culture. *You must put them in a place where you will remember to water them every day,* for ample moisture is the most significant part of their summertime culture.

Winter quarters

In early autumn before cold weather you should move your Azaleas back into winter quarters in your house. Give them a well-lighted spot, and keep them as cool as you can. Coolness during the fall months will enable them to rest until after the first of the year. Then bring them into a warmer room, give them a feeding and more water, and shortly they will be covered with flowers again.

Azaleas in trouble

There are three possible problems with which you may have to contend if you grow Azaleas as house plants throughout the year. The first we shall discuss is "leaf drop." Florist-type Azaleas are evergreens, and, as with all evergreens, there comes a time each year when the oldest leaves will fall. This condition is normal, but when all kinds of leaves—young and old, many of them still green—start to fall, your plant is in real trouble. Leaf drop may be caused by either of two things: lack of sufficient light or not enough water. If your plant has ever been allowed to get bone dry, it will probably lose its leaves and might die. On the other hand, if you know your plant has always had an abundance of moisture, try moving it to a lighter location.

Our next problem is that of red spiders. These very tiny insects build cobwebs under leaves and also suck moisture from them, causing the foliage to turn brownish and brittle. Here, prevention is the best weapon. Wash the foliage of your plants well with cold water under pressure out of doors in the summer, or give them a good sink bath in the wintertime. In the house we simply fill the sink part way with warm sudsy water, tip the plant upside down, holding it in the pot with one hand, and swish it in the water. A few minutes later we do the same operation in clear warm water as a rinse. It really makes house plants look beautiful, and, of course, they do well because bugs, as well as dust, are washed down the drain. If you feel that your plants are so badly infested that an insecticide is needed, try Dimite, one teaspoonful to one gallon of water. Wet the foliage thoroughly with the spray mixture.

You may find that the foliage of your Azaleas gradually becomes light yellowish green with rather noticeable dark green veins. This is not an indication of disease, but of a condition known as *chlorosis* and is a sign that your soil is not acid enough for Azaleas. To restore it to proper acidity, water your plants with a solution made of one ounce of iron sulphate dissolved in two gallons of water. Your druggist has iron sulphate, a very inexpensive chemical, but one which will "put iron in the blood" of your Azaleas. It is a good idea to give your plants a drink of this solution several times a year so that the leaves will always stay a beautiful dark green.

CHAPTER X

Easter's Flower

Oriental migrant

It was nearly one hundred years ago that a storm-battered sailing vessel, crippled by a Caribbean gale, put into St. George's harbor in Bermuda for repairs. Aboard the ship was a missionary, homeward bound after years of service in the Far East. He welcomed the chance to set foot on dry land after the long voyage across the Pacific and around Cape Horn and was particularly pleased when the local rector asked him to be his guest while repairs were made to the ship.

When the day of departure arrived the missionary wanted to repay his host for his hospitality. Aware that money was not appropriate, he thought of the Lily bulbs he had received from a native on an island south of Japan and pressed them on his new friend as a token of his gratitude.

In Bermuda's perpetual spring the Lilies flourished and increased exceedingly in numbers, their snowy flowers and exotic fragrance adding a touch of the Orient to the Atlantic paradise. It was several years later that Mr. W. K. Harris, a nurseryman from Philadelphia visiting on the island, saw the plants. Realizing how much they would be appreciated by his customers, he purchased a number of them and brought them back to the United States.

Today's Easter Lily is much more beautiful than the Harris Lily—its flowers are larger and whiter, its stems are sturdier, and its leaves have more substance—but we can thank Mr. Harris for bringing Easter Lilies into commerce.

How strange Easter decorations would seem if we could not have Easter Lilies.

You don't need a green thumb!

The most inexperienced flower lover can enjoy an Easter Lily as a house plant, since all the work of growing it has been done for him by an expert in the six months which precede Easter. Easter Lilies grow from large scaly bulbs, which have within themselves vast stores of energy. In October of each year florists put Easter Lily bulbs in rich fibrous soil, and from that time until they appear in flower shops, they have daily, almost hourly, care in greenhouses. It is no wonder they are such perfectly beautiful plants at Easter time.

When you buy, or are given, an Easter Lily plant, your only immediate task is to enjoy the plant to the fullest. Take time to inspect your plant closely, observe the perfection of each detail of bud and leaf, and learn from closer communication with this bit of God's world something of the wonder and beauty which surround us in the realm of nature.

Each year after my Easter Lilies have bloomed and faded I find a place for them in my garden, and I urge you to do likewise. One of last year's plants had six flowers at Easter time. This summer in the garden it had twenty-four! Doesn't that give you reason enough to keep your plant growing in the house until it is warm enough to set it outside?

During its stay in the house, plan to give your Easter Lily as much light as you can. Full sun is not necessary, for it will only cause the flower buds to open sooner. Give your plant a light spot and see that the soil beneath it stays moist. It is not necessary to feed it.

Sometimes folk say that the smaller buds on their Easter

Lily plants fail to open in the house. The way to make sure they will mature properly is to syringe the buds and leaves with water occasionally, especially if they are in a hot room.

In order to preserve the snowy whiteness of each Lily flower from pollen stains, florists pluck out the orange stamens as soon as each flower opens. You may easily do the same, or if you prefer, let each flower mature normally with its brilliant stamens dancing in its milk-white chalice.

Salvage operation

The foliage of your Easter Lily is the key to its future well-being, for the leaves manufacture food to be stored in the bulb for another flowering season. Keep your plant growing, in a sunny place if possible, after the flowers fade. When there is no longer a danger from frost plant it in your garden. Choose a well-drained spot where it will get an abundance of sunshine.

Often an Easter Lily will surprise you that first fall by blossoming again. Starting the following summer, however, you may expect flowers each year during the normal flowering season. In my garden they blossom at the same time as the Regal Lilies.

There are certain cold areas where Easter Lilies are not reliably winter hardy. In my garden they have successfully come through 26 degrees below zero weather without winter protection. If you have reason to believe that they may not be hardy in your garden, mulch the soil with several inches of peat moss as a precautionary measure.

CHAPTER XI

Gloxinias — Cousins from Brazil

Latin beauty

How would you like a house plant that could last for twenty years? Some time ago I read about a Gloxinia twenty years old, which had sixty-eight blossoms on it to celebrate its second decade! Here, indeed, is a plant to cling to, not one to throw into the trash barrel simply because this year's flowers have faded!

I say that Gloxinias are cousins from Brazil to dramatize the fact that they are closely related to African Violets, one of the easiest of house plants to grow successfully. Gloxinias, though an ocean apart in origin, do well in surroundings which satisfy the requirements of African Violets. They may even be propagated in the same manner as African Violets, for leaves will root in sand and produce new plants identical in all ways to the plant from which the leaves are taken.

Who's who?

You may be interested to know that the plants we call Gloxinias were involved years ago in a case of mistaken identity, and according to some botanists Gloxinias are not Gloxinias at all. Botanically, Gloxinias are Sinningias; true Gloxinias are perennial plants, also from South America, and have nodding bell-like lavender flowers. Be that as it may, Gloxinias are still Gloxinias to most of us.

Regal splendor

Before telling you how to grow them, I would like for a moment to describe their flowers, though words are poor mortar with which to build Gloxinias! Think of widely fluted trumpets of royal velvet, in colors such as the dyer's hand has never produced. Plantsmen's catalogues describe some of their colors thus: "pansy purple," "raspberry red with white throats," "hyacinth blue," "pure shining white with ruffled edges," "deep glowing pink," "rich dark violet," "bright scarlet," and "honey-colored." In addition, there are varieties whose wide-open faces are sprinkled with what appears to be freckles, or perhaps nutmeg on an apple pie. To complete the Gloxinia picture, imagine the clustered flowers held above rosettes of exotic, fuzzy leaves of deepest green.

Gloxinia life cycle

Gloxinias may be grown from seed or from tubers. Since growing from seed is a rather long and difficult process, we shall not consider that method in this book, but our discussion will be limited to growing them from tubers.

Gloxinias may be had in blossom at any time of the year; however, since there are relatively few good house plants available during the summer months, most florists plan to have the greater part of their Gloxinias mature at that time of year.

Tubers are usually planted in February or early March in a soil rich in organic matter, such as African Violets enjoy. If you start your own tubers, I suggest you use a prepared African Violet Soil, available from your florist or garden center. Commercially, growers use a mixture of two parts leaf mold, one part good loam, and one part peat moss, with a bit of sharp sand added for drainage.

Gloxinias are peculiar in that tubers planted at the same time seldom mature together. There are always a few fast-growing ones, as well as some laggards. This situation is ideal, for it means that from a given planting there will be plants in blossom over an exceptionally long period.

The first indication that the puckered brown tubers intend to be anything more beautiful comes when they send out tiny, fuzzy leaves that look like mouse ears. From that point on they expand in every direction in a most gratifying manner. The leaves hug the soil and soon spread out over the edges of the pots. While the plants are making this leaf growth, feed them every two weeks with a mild solution of a complete house-plant fertilizer.

About the middle of May, from an early March planting, some of the plants will set buds, which will rapidly expand into the glorious flowers I have attempted to describe earlier. You will be amazed at how long Gloxinias will continue to blossom. At the crown of each plant you can easily see the clusters of buds awaiting their turn to open. Use a sharp knife to sever the stems of flowers as they fade. Cut them off low down among the leaves so that no stubs show, and blossoms still to open may do so without interference from those that have withered.

Eventually the time will come when the last flower has come and gone. It is at this point that the differences of growth between Gloxinias and African Violets become apparent. While African Violets, if happy, will continue to flower without ceasing, Gloxinias demand a rest period. You will notice that, shortly after flowering, the leaves look somewhat weather-beaten. Each day thereafter they will retrogress further until they dry up entirely. Now is the time to stop watering and to let the tubers rest. You may set the pots in a warm, dry location until, of their own volition, they start new growth again. Or, after letting the bulbs rest for three or four months, you may start to water them again and force them into growth. At any rate, just as new growth begins, repot your plants in fresh soil. It may be that they will even need larger pots. Use a ready-mixed African Violet Soil. Now the cycle has been completed and you may look forward to your Gloxinia plants' blossoming for you for years without number.

Remember that in the house they will enjoy conditions under which African Violets thrive. Being of tropical origin, they like to be warm, which again is another reason they make good house plants. Do not give them full sun at any time, but do see that they have an abundance of light. A spot on a table near a window protected by thin curtains is ideal, or they will find an east window to their liking, where they can get early-morning sun for a brief period each day.

My last suggestion concerns Gloxinias as gift plants. I am certain that you will enjoy them so much yourself that you will want to share their beauty with others. When you give a Gloxinia you will know that the recipient will have a plant which, when cared for properly, will continue to give joy for years to come.

CHAPTER XII

Why I Like Geraniums

Popularity poll

Someone should run a contest asking participants to write "in twenty-five words or less" why they like a particular flower. No doubt, a large number of the entries would begin: "I like Geraniums because . . ." Few other plants are as dear to the hearts of people throughout the world. It matters not whether you consider a courtyard in Spain or a window sill in Maine; if you find but one blossoming plant, chances are it is a Geranium! All this despite the fact that Geraniums are not particularly good house plants!

Perhaps at this point we should define what we mean by *Geraniums*. Someone has estimated that over one hundred and sixty wild Geranium species from South Africa have been used in producing the varieties we know today, and there are literally hundreds of them, though only about a dozen have proved themselves worthy of a place in commercial floriculture. We are not discussing the Lady Washington or Pansy Geranium, but the common red, white, salmon, or pink ones everyone knows as Geraniums.

Don't expect the impossible

Somehow we feel that these old-fashioned flowers, so much a part of our lives, simply cannot be left to die after a summer's flowering in our gardens. We feel that we must bring them indoors. Now we have arrived at one of the most crucial points to remember. It is too much to ask plants to blossom all summer in our gardens, to stand the shock of uprooting, to adjust themselves to household living, then to continue to blossom all winter, and Geraniums will not do it. If you want to have Geraniums flower on your winter window sill, you must start with fresh plants in late summer.

Geraniums as house plants

Very few florists have Geranium plants to sell in early fall, and yet that is the time you need young plants. Here is how to get them: in June go into your garden and take cuttings from the most free-flowering plants you have. Put the cuttings in moist sand until they root; then pot them up in a not-too-rich soil. Use a soil mixture made up of seven parts loam, three parts peat moss, and two parts sand. A small amount of bone meal added to the mixture will provide all the nutrients needed at potting time.

It is important that your plants be grown in pots all summer long and that all flower buds that form be removed. You must forget about flowers at this stage and concentrate on producing plants which are compact and bushy. You must always keep in mind the fact that Geraniums send out blossoms only from the ends of their stems. If your plants are tall and leggy, with only a stem or two each, then you cannot possibly have many flowers. In order to build up the structure of your plant, pinch back stems often so that they will send out all the side branches possible. Each one of these side branches has a chance of terminating in a cluster of beautiful flowers.

Nothing will take the place of sunshine in the life of a Geranium. You simply must give it the sunniest window sill you have, and if it does not do well there, concede that it is not sunny enough. Haven't you seen Geraniums, tall and gawky, with tufts of tiny leaves at the tops of their stalks like would-be Palm trees? That situation is the result of insufficient light, and if your plants look like that, you should concentrate your efforts on more amenable subjects.

Geraniums are not the easiest house plants to grow, but the large windows of modern homes have made the task much easier than it used to be. I have found Geraniums to be especially satisfactory when grown in a south-facing picture window. No matter where you grow your Geraniums you will find that flowers will appear more abundantly after the turn of the year, when the days become noticeably longer. All flowers are produced only when plants are in active growth; the increased growth sponsored by the spring sun will mean more blossoms on your Geraniums and other house plants as well.

Geraniums may be without flowers and appear to rest at times. When they do not blossom continuously it is because conditions are not suitable for their active growth. This artificial rest period may be brought on by insufficient light, water, or food. Of these factors, lack of enough light is most apt to be the limiting one.

CHAPTER XIII

Chrysanthemums — Autumn's Golden Harvest

Floral heritage

For the last two thousand autumns of recorded history Chrysanthemums have delighted the hearts of men. Ancient Chinese gardeners tamed the wild Chrysanthemums of the hillsides at an early time, and when Western explorers first visited that country, they found the autumn gardens of Cathay adorned with both single- and double-flowering varieties in many colors. More than one thousand years ago the Japanese adopted a stylized Chrysanthemum flower as their imperial emblem. Few flowers have been a part of men's lives for as many centuries.

Changing nature's ways

The pungent fragrance of Chrysanthemums and their coloring, so much akin to the golds and russets of our autumn woodlands, make them the choicest flowers of the season. Flower lovers of this and coming generations will forget that until a few years ago Chrysanthemums could be enjoyed only during the fall of the year because nowadays florists have them to sell at every season. The secret of year-round Chrysanthemum culture was discovered by men who probed into the value of light to various plants. Some plants, they found, would flower regardless of the number of hours of daylight they received. Others would blossom only as the days became longer. Chrysanthemums were in the third group of plants whose flower buds formed only as days became shorter.

With that knowledge at their command, they had only

to take the step to what is now called "black shading," an example of which is this: a variety of Chrysanthemum which normally would blossom in November, let us say, can be covered with opaque cloth in midsummer from 5 P.M. until 7 A.M., giving the plants fourteen hours of night and ten hours of day, corresponding to late autumn conditions. The plants respond by setting flower buds and are often in full blossom as much as two months ahead of season.

Then came the advent of lighting plants in winter months. During short winter days Chrysanthemums try to make flowers, even though they are only a few inches tall. Now they are given artificial light for several hours a day, in effect making January days as long as July ones as far as the plants are concerned. Thus on they grow, taller and taller. When they become tall enough the lights are taken away, and within a short time the plants start to blossom.

The refinements of this system are multitudinous, with certain varieties performing better at one season than at others. The fact remains that, from the point of view of flower consumers, Chrysanthemums are now considered year-round pot plants and cut flowers.

One of the nice things about pot-grown Chrysanthemums, in addition to their beauty and fabulous longevity, is the fact that they are among the most inexpensive plants on the market. Use pot plants of Chrysanthemums often, not only in your own home, but as gifts to friends in hospitals, for example. They stand up beautifully with a minimum of care.

Care of pot-grown Chrysanthemums

All living plants need light, and Chrysanthemums are no exception. You will find, for instance, that if you leave your Chrysanthemum plants in a dark place, the leaves will soon turn yellow, beginning with those closest to the ground. Even under these conditions, however, the flowers still remain beautiful, though new ones opening are apt to be paler in color than flowers grown in the light. If possible, give your Chrysanthemum plants some sunshine every day. If you cannot arrange for adequate light, enjoy the plants anyway, for they will still stay lovely much longer than a bouquet of cut flowers.

Chrysanthemum plants use a great deal of moisture each day, especially under the warm conditions found in most homes; so you must water them diligently. If you do, they will last for an exceptionally long time.

Something for nothing

I have not told you before, but with pot-grown Chrysanthemums there is often a hidden bonus, which you may collect by planting them in your garden after the flowers fade. All varieties are not hardy in gardens, and all will not do well, but any plants you have are worth a try. Usually the small-flowered varieties do better in the garden than large-flowered ones. We have often seen pot-grown Chrysanthemums, sold in full flower at Mother's Day in May, have another crop of blossoms in the garden a few months later as normal autumn weather re-establishes their age-old blossoming schedule!

CHAPTER XIV

Hydrangeas in the Springtime

A certain sign that spring is coming is the appearance of the first magnificently flowered Hydrangeas in florists' windows. Their flower heads are usually six to eight inches in diameter and often much larger than that. It may be that you have heard them called French Hydrangeas and assumed that they came from France. As a matter of fact, florists' Hydrangeas are native to China and Japan and in those countries have been garden plants for hundreds of years. The word *French* in the name has its legitimate place, however, in that for many years new and improved varieties were bred in France and sold to greenhouse operators all over the world.

Hydrangeas may be any shade of pink through orchid and lavender to blue and purple, as well as pure white. They are normally pink, and the various shades of blue are the result of the addition of aluminum to the soil in which they are growing. It is generally true that the deeper the blue or purple color, the greater the aluminum concentration in the soil. Florists have found that some varieties "blue up" better than others, and they have also found that the white varieties are unaffected by any attempt to change their color.

Along about Easter time, when florists' windows are banked with snowy Lilies and masses of pink and blue Hydrangeas, it is hard to resist the urge to buy at least one of these colorful plants for oneself, or to give to someone else. Let us start our cultural notes with the moment your sales resistance has been overcome by your need for beauty, and you say, "I'll take that one!"

Water! Water! Water!

Regardless of the number of flowers on your plants, you will immediately be impressed by the size of the plant in proportion to the size of the pot in which it is growing. The leaves will be huge, and it is in recognition of this fact that this Hydrangea is known botanically as *Hydrangea macrophylla*, "the Hydrangea with the large leaves." These large leaves need a prodigious amount of water each day, and if you learn no other lesson from this text, remember that your Hydrangea must never be allowed to dry out. In order to assuage its thirst you may have to water it more than once a day. If by chance you forget to water it, and it wilts badly, immerse the entire pot in a pail of water for a few minutes so that the soil becomes saturated. Then take the plant out and set it in a shady spot. In an hour you will be amazed at how it has recovered. Of course, this assumes that your plant has not been allowed to dry out to the point of death before you try to resurrect it.

A Hydrangea will often stay in flower for six to eight weeks. In order to keep it lovely for the longest possible time, find a spot for it where it will receive an abundance of light, but not full sun. That should be easy to do, whether you protect it from the sun by thin curtains, or whether you simply place it back a bit from the window. It is not necessary to feed your Hydrangea, since it was given sufficient food, while being grown by your florist, to see it through to maturity.

Garden bound

The time will come when your Hydrangea will have finished flowering. Knowing the intricate timing and skill necessary to bring it into flower in a greenhouse, I recommend that you do not try to carry your plant over in the house. Instead, find a place for it in your garden, and you will have the plant there for an indefinite number of years. There is a factor about growing Hydrangeas in gardens that cannot be overlooked; that is, Hydrangeas are not hardy everywhere. From the vicinity of southern Connecticut southward, they become large garden shrubs, sometimes five to six feet tall, but in the more northern states they will kill back to the ground each year. If you live in a cold climate, treat your plant in one of two ways. Either let it die down each year and treat it as a herbaceous perennial, contenting yourself with a yearly display of luxuriant foliage, or endeavor to protect your plant by covering it. A heavy mulch of straw is sufficient in some areas, but a mound of earth covering the entire plant is a more certain protection. It must be remembered that the buds which will make blossoms are the large ones at the tips of the stems. If they are pruned off or allowed to winterkill, you will not get any flowers.

Pink or blue?

Perhaps you have wondered why some Hydrangeas are pink and others blue. As we have pointed out, the availability of aluminum, present in most soils, governs Hydrangea colors. Soil scientists have shown that pink flowers will be produced as long as the soil is nearly neutral so that aluminum in the soil will remain in a chemical combination that the plants cannot assimilate. When Hydrangeas are grown in an acid soil, they are able to absorb aluminum, and the flowers become some shade of blue. In commercial practice the pink flowers are produced by maintaining the soil pH at about 6.5 (nearly neutral) during the fall growing period prior to greenhouse forcing. When blue flowers are desired, alum, at the rate of one teaspoonful to a five-inch pot, is applied to the soil during the early part of the greenhouse forcing period. This lowers the soil pH below 6.0, making it more acid, and supplies the aluminum necessary for the blue flowers. The shade of blue depends upon the amount of the aluminum the plants absorb. Perhaps this brief glimpse behind the scenes, showing some of the factors which florists must consider in growing their crops, will serve to show the skill that is necessary to produce the flowers we have come to accept as commonplace. In your garden you may have blue Hydrangeas by keeping the soil acid with applications of alum, or pink flowers by increasing the alkalinity of the soil with ground limestone.

CHAPTER XV

Picking the Good Foliage Plants

Only a horticulturist can really appreciate the change
that has taken place recently in the realm of foliage plants.
It used to be that every plant in commerce was neatly
catalogued. All one had to do was to consult Bailey's *En-
cyclopedia of Horticulture* if there was any question to be
answered.

How times have changed! Recently a plant hunter returned from Japan with over seven hundred live plants,
four hundred of which were unknown to commercial horticulture. Again and again trade journals tell of expeditions
to Africa, Central America, Peru, or the Philippines, con-
ducted by men who intend to introduce new plants to our
homes and gardens.

Strangely enough, most of the area being visited nowadays has been covered many times by other plantsmen
for the last century or more. The difference is that the
earlier explorations were made in the hope of finding new
varieties of flowering plants, particularly Orchids. The
vines and shrubs that impeded former travelers, and which
they slashed unmercifully with their machetes, are the ob-
jectives of today's plant hunters!

The basic reason these travels to exotic lands are fi-
nancially worth while is that we plant buyers today are
demanding something unusual and different from the common English Ivy and Sansevieria. We are intrigued by the
fact that we can grow jungle plants in our own living
rooms. We are fascinated by the odd colorations of the
leaves and stems and by the unfamiliar leaf patterns and
growth habits. We are finding that modern homes with

their wide expanses of glass are almost conservatory-like in their ability to satisfy the needs of these newer plants.

Modern decorators were quick to grasp the possibilities inherent in the new architecture. Living plants have become another tool in their magic chest. Every new building seems to have provision nowadays for green plants to enhance its beauty. Restaurants or skyscrapers, model homes or new insurance offices, all have a place for foliage plants as part of their integral design. Now to the plants themselves!

You can grow a Philodendron

It is only fair that we begin our discussion with Philodendrons, for they are among the easiest of all foliage plants to grow, and at least one variety of Philodendron is to be found in every flower shop in the land. As to their popularity, it is an accepted fact that more plants of Heartleaf Philodendron (*Philodendron cordatum*) are sold each year than any other plant. Of course, the real reason this is so is because people have found that they can make them grow in their homes. That very fact, that they will grow in almost any home, ought to be the theme of our discussion of Philodendrons. They prefer a spot just out of the sun, yet with abundant light; however, they are extremely tolerant and will exist for a long while in places so dimly lighted that other plants would succumb within a few days.

One of my friends who has a particularly dark mantel has two sets of Philodendrons. Every few days she takes the ones from the mantel to a spot closer to a window and takes those from the window to the mantel. Even receiving light on a half-time basis, all the plants remain perfectly healthy.

Some folk suggest that the soil beneath Philodendrons should be allowed to dry between waterings, but I feel that you should resort to this only if you want to keep a plant from growing too large. Keep the soil just damp, not saturated. Philodendrons in warm houses give off moisture from their leaves at all times, and it is only right that there be some water in the soil, from which they can draw as they need it.

Philodendron cordatum, the Heartleaf Philodendron, is the easiest plant of all to grow. There are forms with larger leaves than others. They may be used as trailing plants in hanging containers, or they may be grown upright upon supports, to which they will cling as they climb.

Philodendron panduraeforme is a beautiful waxy-leaved variety somewhat larger than the Heartleaf Philodendron. Its leaves are generally three-lobed, with the center lobe much longer than the side ones. This Philodendron should be grown on a support of some kind. Florists grow upright Philodendrons on what they call "totem poles." Totem poles are simply slabs of bark, tree fern, or some other material into which the climbing plants can send their roots for support as they climb. It is interesting to note that as soon as Philodendrons reach the stage of climbing, they seem to grow much more vigorously than before.

Philodendron hastatum is a magnificent climbing plant whose dark green leaves are shaped like gigantic spear points. The stem is thick, and from it the plant sends out numerous roots by which it clings to trees in the jungle or to a totem pole in your home.

The last climbing Philodendron I want to mention is not really a Philodendron, although it is often sold as one. The Swiss Cheese Plant is sold as *Philodendron pertusum* when young, for at that time its leaves are relatively small and without perforations. As it gets larger (and it grows to immense proportions), the mature leaf character asserts itself, showing the familiar Swiss-cheese effect. Then the plant is called *Monstera deliciosa*. Of course, it has been a *Monstera* all along—how confusing!

Now we come to some of the most exciting of the new Philodendrons, those which do not climb. Horticulturally they are known as "self-heading" Philodendrons. Perhaps it would be better to say that they are basal branching. In other words, they do not form a climbing stem but send all of their leaves forth from a central crown. Their usefulness lies in the fact that they do not grow up tall and lanky like the climbing types, but instead become broader, more beautiful specimens. There are two forms readily available at flower shops nowadays, *Philodendron Wendlandi* and *Philodendron selloum*, and in a few years there will be many more.

Philodendron Wendlandi is one of the choicest house plants known. Its leaves are spatulate or long oval in shape and from one to two feet in length. The foliage is glossy, and altogether the plant is exceedingly attractive. In order to display this magnificent plant so that its bold leaf character is at its best, one should be sure that each plant has sufficient room to grow without crowding.

Philodendron selloum is a cut-leaf, self-heading variety. Its habit of growth is more spreading than *P. Wendlandi*, and it is extremely exotic in appearance. To be considered also is the fact that *P. selloum* will tolerate cool locations very well, much better than most foliage plants.

No doubt, someone is going to wonder why I have not included other Philodendrons in my list of good foliage plants. The reason is simple. Although botanists recognize over two hundred and fifty species of Philodendrons, only about one third of these are to be found even in fanciers' collections. I have made a list of representative types, all of which may be found at reasonable prices in flower shops. There are other Philodendrons to be found in commerce, but as yet they are not widely distributed. It is well to remember that all Philodendrons make good house plants and that they are especially useful in locations where good light is not available.

The Fig family

If I remember the story correctly, Fig trees were growing in the Garden of Eden, which means they have been with us for a long time. What is not generally understood, however, is that the Fig family is a very diversified one. In addition to the edible Figs there are others which creep along the ground and some, like the Banyan of India (*Ficus benghalensis*), that claim to be among the world's largest living things.

There are three members of the Fig family especially suited for house culture. I particularly endorse the one known as Fiddle-leaf Fig (*Ficus pandurata* or *Ficus lyrata*). Here is a plant which is almost indestructible, whose large fiddle-shaped leaves are glossy and disease free. Fiddle-leaf Figs will grow in almost any soil, wet or dry, and can tolerate either full sun or dense shade. Naturally, a good fertile soil, combined with an abundance of light and moisture, will produce the best plants. In tropical Africa, Fiddle-leaf Figs are forest trees and often grow to be forty feet tall.

Ficus elastica or India Rubber Plant, a real old-timer in horticulture, is my next selection. This is the one which has been a favorite in barbershop and restaurant windows for many generations. There are varieties with green and white foliage, but usually the green-leaved plants are more satisfactory. In India and Malaya, where this species is a native tree, it often becomes one hundred feet in height. *Ficus elastica* will tolerate sun or shade and should be kept moderately moist.

The last Fig included in this group is a tiny evergreen creeper known as *Ficus radicans variegata*. This little plant has beautiful green and white leaves not over two inches long, which are rough to the touch. It may be grown as a hanging plant or as a climber for a totem pole. Ordinary soil, some protection from the sun, and average moisture will keep this little beauty happy.

Peperomias

Most of the foliage plants discussed thus far have been large-growing types. Now we come to Peperomias, whose stature varies from two inches to about a foot in height. Some green-plant specialists grow a dozen or more kinds of Peperomias, but here we shall discuss them only as a group. All Peperomias are wonderful house plants. All have excellent foliage, ranging from the mouse-eared size of P. *minima* through the dark beauty of Emerald Ripple to the large, silver-streaked leaves of the Watermelon Begonia, known correctly as *Peperomia Sandersii*.

Grow Peperomias somewhat on the dry side and give them protection from the sun. Peperomias will last for years as house plants and each summer favor you with their version of flowers, tiny rat-tailed spikes of cream-white blossoms. Most of the Peperomias grown as house plants are native to tropical sections of South America.

Dracaenas are tough

Among the more tolerant of house plants we surely should include the Dracaenas. Although they seem so unlike Lilies, botanists tell us that they are truly members of that family of plants. There are a great many different kinds of Dracaenas to be had as house plants, but we shall discuss only two readily available varieties.

Dracaena Godseffiana is an amazing plant with dark

green leaves, which appear to have been sprinkled with gold dust. The leaves are borne in whorls of three on wiry stems. This Dracaena rarely grows over a foot tall; so it makes a fine house plant. It grows best in a warm location (up to 80 degrees) where there is filtered light. Try to keep the soil from becoming excessively wet or dry.

Dracaena Sanderiana appears to be as unlike *Dracaena Godseffiana* as two plants can be, yet they are closely related, botanically speaking. The most apt description of *Dracaena Sanderiana* would be to say that it looks like a stalk of corn except that the leaves have white margins. Both Dracaenas are native to the Congo region of Africa. Culture is the same for each of them.

There are many other members of the Dracaena family and a related species known as *Cordyline*, all of which make fine house plants. They require a minimum of care and last for many years. You might be interested to know that the Hawaiian Ti plant, so easily grown from stem segments, is *Cordyline terminalis*. Great quantities of its lovely foliage, tinged with red and purple, are used by florists in exotic flower arrangements.

Australian Umbrella Tree (*Schefflera actinophylla*)

Whenever I talk about Scheffleras I have to be careful, or superlatives will surely creep into my discussion! Nature has endowed this lovely house plant with foliage very similar in shape to that of Virginia Creeper. Botanists call each leaf digitately compound because the various segments arise from a central point, just as our fingers spread out from the palms of our hands.

Young Schefflera leaves are so shiny they appear to be coated with varnish, *wet varnish* at that. Under artificial light they glisten as though recently moistened with dew.

They are large-growing house plants, but they attain their stature slowly.

Scheffleras are tolerant of a wide range of temperatures, but do best under the same warm conditions we enjoy in our own homes. Protect them from the midday sun, and keep the soil beneath them moderately moist.

Dieffenbachia

In the interest of simplification I shall group all Dieffenbachias together, since those commercially available are all quite similar. Dieffenbachias are upright-growing foliage plants with huge leaves commonly mottled with patches of pale green or white. Individual leaves are often a foot long and half as wide.

As Dieffenbachias increase in age, their one central stem becomes taller, and the older leaves fade and drop off. Eventually the plants become gawky, but this can be overcome by cutting off the tip and rooting it in sand. Pot it in a mixture of half soil and half peat moss, and you will have a fine, low, compact plant again. Incidentally, if a stem is cut into sections and the pieces are laid on their sides and barely covered with moist peat, many new plants will arise, which also can be potted individually as noted above.

Grow Dieffenbachias under average household temperatures and they will respond favorably. Do not overwater, but allow the soil to become nearly dry between waterings.

It is interesting to note that Dieffenbachias are sometimes called Dumb Cane. If a bit of the juice from a Dieffenbachia is applied to the tip of one's tongue, the tongue soon loses its sensitivity and a person finds it extremely difficult, or impossible, to talk.

English Ivy

No house-plant collection would be complete without at least one representative of the newer forms of English Ivy. The species *Hedera helix* is infrequently grown nowadays as a house plant, chiefly because its leaves are so large and widely spaced as compared with those varieties of more recent introduction.

There are dozens of fine English Ivies on the market today, and they are all extremely easy to grow. A sampling of names will give you an intriguing insight into the possibilities of using today's English Ivy in your house. Here are a dozen varieties picked at random: Green Ripples, California Branching, Pixie, Heart-leaf, Shamrock, Ruffled, Miniature Variegated, Glacier, Pittsburgh, Hahn's Self-branching, Gold Dust, and Maple Queen.

Grow English Ivies in strong light and do not overwater. They do well as trailing plants and as climbers also if given a small support. The easiest way to keep English Ivies healthy is to give your plants a bath each week. A dip in warm sudsy water, followed by a clear rinse, will keep the foliage clean and glowing with vitality.

Rex Begonias

Old-fashioned flowers have a way of returning to popularity almost overnight. Rex Begonias are current examples of the whims of flower lovers. There are many varieties of Rex Begonias, but all are characterized by having large, soft-textured leaves usually marked with spots or bands of silver against a reddish-green background. Often the undersides of the leaves and the leaf stems are an even darker shade of reddish green.

Give these lovely plants protection from the sun, yet see that they receive an abundance of light. They should be grown in a light sandy soil to which about one third peat moss has been added. Do not be too generous in watering Rex Begonias, but let the soil become moderately dry between waterings.

That they are tough house plants is evidenced by one of my own, which has been in the same flowerpot for at least five years and still looks beautiful. Each year it sends up graceful sprays of pale pink flowers as an added attraction. My plant gets mild feedings of a complete house-plant fertilizer three or four times a year.

If you want additional plants of a Rex Begonia, simply take a leaf and lay it on moist sand in a covered glass dish, after cutting entirely through the leaf veins in several places. Within a few weeks new plants will spring up wherever the veins were cut.

It may interest you to know that Rex Begonias are native to Assam. When they were first introduced to England many years ago, someone exclaimed, "They are Begonias fit for a king," or words to that effect, and their name, Rex Begonias, came into being.

Xanthosoma Lindeni

It would seem that someone should find a name less tongue twisting and pretentious than *Xanthosoma Lindeni* for a pretty little house plant! Nevertheless, Xanthosoma seems to be as much of a nickname as we can find for this newly introduced house plant from Columbia.

At first glance you might think that a Xanthosoma is a Caladium, and you would be nearly right, for they are closely related. Both grow from a similar type of root, and both have large attractive leaves of much the same shape. A Xanthosoma's leaves are more sagittate, or arrowhead shaped, and are bright green with clear white veins and midribs.

Grow this lovely plant in a shady place for best results, and feed it monthly with a mild complete fertilizer.

Wax Plant

All good foliage plants are not necessarily new introductions. *Hoya carnosa,* the Wax Plant, has been delighting flower lovers for generations. Wax Plants are climbing or trailing vines according to the way they are trained.

Their leaves are extremely thick and heavy and may be dull green or green and white, depending upon the variety. The real reason for growing Wax Plants is for the fragrant beauty of their waxy pink flowers. The flowers are borne in clusters from tiny spurs, which arise from the stems. Do not cut off the spurs after the flowers fade because new flowers will arise from the same places year after year.

Wax Plants are averse to moist conditions; so water them sparingly. They are tolerant of a wide range of light conditions. They will grow in dimly lighted spots and in places that are extremely bright and hot as well.

Kangaroo Ivy and Grape Ivy

The last two foliage plants I shall call to your attention are vines known botanically as *Cissus.* The Kangaroo Ivy, *Cissus antarctica,* is one of the most long-suffering house plants you can hope to find. Even under the most adverse conditions it will continue to send forth new foliage as though you were lavishing all your attention on it alone. The Kangaroo Ivy has lovely dark green leaves three to four inches long, saw-toothed on their edges.

Grape Ivy, *Cissus rhombifolia,* has three-parted leaves somewhat the shape of Poison Ivy foliage. It requires a bit more light than Kangaroo Ivy and seems to appreciate regular feedings.

The care of leaves of foliage plants

A few years ago it would not have been necessary to write this message about the care of leaves. At that time everyone washed the leaves of their plants with water and thought that they were doing a good job. Contrary to much that is heard today, they were right!

Let us begin this discussion about leaves with a short refresher course in elementary botany. If you will remember, leaves are the very complex factories within which all of the fuel we use is, or in ancient times was, manufactured. Coal and oil, for example, are the end products of vegetation which grew on the earth in prehistoric times. Likewise, all the food used by man and beast was herbage at one time though it may now appear to us as milk or meat. The Bible states the truth succinctly when in Isaiah 40:6 it says, "All flesh is grass." Photosynthesis, the manufacture of food in leaves by the action of chlorophyll in the presence of sunlight, is one process man has not yet been able to duplicate. It is too close to the source of life itself.

Leaves, in themselves, are magnificently intricate mechanisms composed of many layers of cells. The outer layer, called the epidermis, covers each leaf completely, top and bottom. Most of its cells are composed largely of a waxy material known as cutin. This cutinous layer is very tough and resists the passage of water or gases. The relative impermeability of this thin layer of cells is what protects plants from dying when water is not constantly available to them.

There has to be an arrangement, however, so that plants may breathe. This function is taken care of by specialized cells in the epidermis known as guard cells. They are crescent-shaped cells, arranged in pairs, which open and close the tiny openings in the leaves that are the passageways for the interchange of oxygen, carbon dioxide, and water vapor between the outside air and the internal leaf cells. It would be difficult to imagine any cells of a plant which are of more vital importance to its well-being. The openings guarded by the cells are known as stomata, and it is the activity of these cells that is the real object of this entire discussion, for without the use of their stomata plants literally suffocate.

Stomata may be found on the tops of leaves or on the undersides of leaves. Usually there are relatively few to be found on the upper sides of leaves, for almost all plants concentrate the greatest number of their stomata on the lower surfaces. A notable exception is a plant like a Water Lily, whose leaves lie upon the surface of the water. In the scheme of things a Water Lily has all its stomata on the top side!

It has become customary for many people to apply a substance of some sort to the leaves of their foliage plants to make them shiny. If the plant being treated happens to be an India Rubber Plant, their action may be done with relative impunity provided the material is applied to the top surfaces of the leaves only, for this particular kind of plant has all its stomata on the bottom sides of its leaves. If the bottoms are covered too, the stomata may become clogged and useless and the plant may die.

Horticulture seems to have more than its share of fads, and one of the current ones is to make the leaves of plants shiny, whether or not they were endowed by nature with this characteristic. Not long ago a lady brought to a garden-club meeting at which I was lecturing a leaf from a huge Philodendron, which appeared to have been burned in some way. Upon inquiry I found that she had carefully rubbed each leaf of her plants with olive oil. Every plant in a huge collection that had cost her two hundred dollars was dead. So much for olive oil!

Do not confuse these materials that make leaves shine with foliar feeding. Scientists have found that diluted concentrations of chemicals can be taken into plant leaves advantageously under certain circumstances. Such a practice is entirely different from that which has been discussed above.

Perhaps I should state clearly that I am a believer in enjoying plants as they grow without "gilding the Lily." It may well be that some substances may be applied to leaves without apparent injury, but I, for one, will let the decision be Nature's, not mine!

When foliage plants stop growing

Sometimes the question is asked as to whether or not foliage plants rest. The answer is an intricate one because the plants themselves come from widely separated parts of the world. No one answer can apply to all of them.

Plants of the Temperate Zones of the world have definite growth and rest periods, corresponding with warm and cold seasons. In the tropics, where temperatures are always mild, there are some sections where rainfall patterns create wet and dry seasons; thus plants grow or rest according to the availability of moisture.

The majority of the foliage plants in our homes, however, come from areas of the tropics where there is continuous growth. Philodendrons, for instance, will grow indefinitely as long as temperature and moisture conditions are right. If foliage plants seem to rest in our homes, it is usually because we fail to meet their growth needs. Being tough, they can remain attractive for long periods of time, but to keep them as permanent residents we must provide an environment that meets their needs.

CHAPTER XVI

Less Common House Plants

In this book considerable space has been devoted to plants which are commonly available at flower shops throughout the year. Now we shall discuss in a more limited way the culture of other plants that are grown in smaller quantities each season. This does not mean that these flowers are less desirable or that they are less beautiful. Some of them are rather small plants; others have a short period of flowering; certain ones are not grown everywhere because of climatic limitations; and some are varieties which were grown in large quantities years ago, but are produced in fewer numbers today.

Calceolarias

Years ago a plant-hunting expedition exploring the Andes Mountains of Peru and Chile found Calceolarias twelve feet tall with pouch-like blossoms as large as hens' eggs. Although the ancestors of all our Calceolarias originated in this region, these giants surely did not enter into the breeding of today's plants. Our Calceolarias usually grow about ten or twelve inches high, though sometimes a bit more. Their flowers are a shade of yellow, bronze, pink, or red with an abundance of spots of brown or purple on all the flowers. The name *Calceolaria* is derived from the Latin *calceolus*, alluding to the likeness of its flowers to slippers. Sometimes they are called Pocketbook Flowers in another attempt to describe their unusual blossoms.

There are two main types of Calceolarias grown as pot plants. One is the herbaceous kind, grown from seed each year. Its habit of growth is short and squat, and its flowers are large and heavily spotted. The other type is somewhat shrubby in nature. It is usually grown from cuttings rather than from seed. Although its flowers are very small in comparison with the first variety mentioned, they make up the difference by sheer weight of numbers. This type of Calceolaria is inclined to grow somewhat taller than the first variety, and its flowers have fewer spots. Individual flowers of the first variety are often an inch or more across, while those of the second type grow about the size of a penny.

In their native land Calceolarias grow where it is cool and moist and where the rays of the sun are tempered by a perpetual foggy overcast. This fact, translated into household terms, indicates that Calceolarias will do best when grown in a place protected from the sun and as cool as possible. They need light but they cannot stand the full fury of the sun itself. Also it means that, in order for them to be happy, it is necessary that the soil beneath them stay moist. It is much more satisfactory to water them from below, by putting water into a saucer, than to try to pour it among the leaves, which hug the tops of the pots very closely.

Calceolarias are strictly spring-flowering pot plants and may be had, in the regions where they are grown, from February until May. I say "in the regions where they are grown" because in order for Calceolarias to set flower buds they must have about three months of temperatures below 60 degrees. That rules them out of greenhouses south of 35 degrees latitude unless they are grown at a high, cool altitude.

Treat Calceolarias as annuals by discarding them when the flowers fade.

Cinerarias

In name, Cinerarias and Calceolarias are somewhat the same, and the type of culture they require is similar also, but when flowers are compared, all semblance ceases. Cineraria blossoms are like huge clusters of Daisies, but such Daisies as you have never seen! Some clusters are as much as a foot across. The Daisy-like flowers seem to be made of the richest royal velvet known. Their colors may be pastel or intense, shading from pure white through blush and pink, on to blue and a purple so deep as to seem unreal. There is no doubt about it, you will like Cinerarias!

There is only one bit of awkwardness: Will Cinerarias like you? They must be grown in a bright, cool location and must never be allowed to dry out. If you have a room where the temperature does not rise above 65 degrees, you can really enjoy Cinerarias. Their flowering season is from December to May, though no one plant lasts that long. Water them from below so as not to wet their foliage. Wet leaves sometimes encourage a stem rot, making the entire plant wilt and die even though moist.

Treat Cinerarias as annuals. When their flowers finally fade discard the plants and get new ones to replace them.

Primroses

There are over three hundred known wild species of Primroses, but these notes will mention only the *three* types best suited for use as house plants. Most people like the Fairy Primrose best of all. This native of China is known as *Primula malacoides,* and from it has been developed several improved strains with larger flowers and clearer colors than the original wild species. You will like it too as soon as you see its delicate pink or white flowers dancing on tiered whorls like something from the land of make-believe. The Fairy Primrose blossoms for several weeks and may be found in flower shops from December until April.

The second type I shall discuss also originated in China and is known as *Primula obconica*. This Primrose you may remember having seen in flower shops during the winter months. Its flowers are often as large as silver dollars and are usually some shade of pink.

Obconica Primroses have one blot on their record, which has unfortunately become associated erroneously with other Primroses as well. Some persons develop a rash or skin irritation from handling Obconica Primroses. Why they should affect some people and not others is hard to understand. Despite this fact, they are still grown in great numbers because those who know of their beauty continue to demand them.

The last Primrose in our trio is the Polyanthus Primrose, whose hybrid background consists of several species, including the true English Primrose. The Polyanthus is the common Primrose grown in gardens, and some readers will be surprised to see it included in a book about house plants. Nevertheless, it makes a good inexpensive small plant which supplies the breath of spring all of us need when winter snows are deep. Polyanthus Primroses, of course, should find a place in your garden after their stint as house plants. There they will multiply and become more beautiful with each passing year.

We have purposely not mentioned the house culture of Primroses until now, for all of them should be treated alike. They enjoy spring weather, which means cool temperatures. They like light, all you can provide in midwinter, though full sun is not necessary. The soil beneath them must be always moist, but not saturated.

That is all there is to taking care of them—just enjoy

them. There is sufficient nourishment in each pot of soil to see the plant through. The Fairy Primroses and the Obconicas should be thrown out when flowers fade, but the Polyanthuses should be grown on until weather is mild enough for them to go into your garden.

Primroses are not expensive, and they blossom for long weeks without ceasing, especially the first two varieties mentioned. Imagine a row of Fairy Primroses on a window sill, framed by fluffy white curtains. Such a sight in a guest room surely spells "welcome" to those who come to visit.

Amaryllis

It is common knowledge that Dutch horticulturists have a way with bulbs, both envied and emulated by their contemporaries in other lands. Their skill in growing Tulips and Hyacinths has, no doubt, given them special abilities with which to draw out the finest characteristics of Amaryllis also.

Amaryllis, as we know them today, are all hybrids whose ancestors grew wild near the Dutch colonies at the Cape of Good Hope. Back in the Netherlands the wildlings underwent exciting transformations so that today we have Amaryllis whose red, pink, or striped Lily-like flowers sometimes measure over one foot across! Other sections of the world, notably Florida and California, produce bulbs equal to any nowadays, but that magic name *Dutch* still conveys a meaning of extra quality.

There are very few house plants that are as easy to grow as Amaryllis. The only thing is, you must learn a few new rules! Let us begin our Amaryllis year in October, for it is then that the bulbs are dug from the growing fields and begin to appear in flower shops and garden centers. At first glance you will probably be surprised at how large Amaryllis bulbs are. Next, you will probably doubt me when I say that you should plant them so that two thirds of each bulb sticks above the surface of the soil in your flowerpot. Finally, I am going to advise you to plant them in flowerpots so small that there is not over an inch of space left around the bulbs from their outer edges to the inside edges of the pots. See, I told you there would be new rules!

Amaryllis like a heavy soil. One composed of two parts of heavy loam and one part of cow manure is satisfactory. To each pot add one teaspoonful of bone meal well mixed with the soil. Use a stick when potting your bulbs so as to firm the soil around them well, but at the same time treat their roots gently. Be careful not to cut or crush them.

After potting, give your plants a big drink of water, and thereafter, until new growth appears, keep the soil barely moist. As soon as the new shoots appear, increase the amount of water you give them.

During the time from potting until growth starts, light is not important, but from that point forward your plants should have full sun. You will be delighted and amazed at how fast they will grow. You can actually measure the amount from day to day with a ruler. Sometimes plants send forth leaves and flowers simultaneously, but more often the flower spike arises first. On large bulbs a second spike with fewer, but no less beautiful, flowers often appears about the time the first one fades.

After flowering, each Amaryllis sends out long straplike leaves, whose job it is to replenish the bulb's strength for another year. Feed the plants bimonthly with a dilute house-plant fertilizer to encourage these leaves to do their job well. When weather becomes mild, set them outside in a sunny place so that they may continue to grow all summer long. In the fall before frost, return them to the house and keep them quite dry until after Christmas. Then water more frequently and you will have flowers all over again.

AMARYLLIS AFTER THEIR DISPLAY

Now that they have stopped blooming, everyone wants to know how to care for their bulbs. If you want to try to make your amaryllis bloom again next winter, cut the plant stalk down to 1". Stake the leaves and let them grow in a bright spot where they will get at least 2 or 3 hours of sun or bright light. Water about once a week and fertilize. After the danger of frost has passed, put them outside on your porch or in your garden where they will get some bright light or sun. In the fall, before that first frost, bring them in, cut off the leaves, let the soil dry out, and put them, pot and all, in a box and place in s cool place like your garage or your outside storage closet. After at least 6 weeks, bring them back in to warmth and light, and water about once a week. Watch for new growth. Good luck!   *Fran Herbert*

WD-40 FOR THE BODY

Is your body feeling a bit rusty after a long winter of physical restrictions? Is your mobility limited by arthritis pain, feeling off-balance, or just lack of use? Accompanied by spirited music from around the world, we gently and rhythmically move all joints in the body with a variety of movement forms drawn from martial arts, dancing arts and healing arts. No matter your age or condition, each movement is easily adapted to individual needs and abilities. Oh, yeah. And we have fun, too.

On Mondays from 9-9:45 in the Studio at the Wellness Center, led by Patricia Higgins, Nia instructor

Reserve your spot by phoning The Wellness Center at 653-8577.

Patricia Higgins

THANK YOU FOR CHRYSANTHI'S ART

Be sure to look at the latest art

DAHLIAS

CALADIUM

FLORISTS' "MUM"

SPIDER CHRYSANTHEMUM

CLUSTER VARIETY CHRYSANTHEMUMS

DAISY-FLOWERED CHRYSANTHEMUMS

SWEETHEART ROSE

HYBRID TEA ROSES

VICTORIAN BOUQUET

AUTUMN FLOWERS

THANKSGIVING ARRANGEMENT

HOLLY FOR THE CHRISTMAS SEASON

POINSETTIAS

At the beginning of the second season, instead of repotting, simply scratch out as much soil as you can around the bulbs and put in fresh soil along with a teaspoonful of bone meal. Repot Amaryllis bulbs every three years.

Amaryllis produce some of the largest flowers of any cultivated plant, and they will do it on your window sill with no more care than has been outlined above. Some persons will not read these remarks until long after the normal Amaryllis-planting season. To them I suggest a visit to a flower shop. Perhaps they will find an Amaryllis just ready to open its blossoms!

Tuberous-rooted Begonias

It would be a mistake to say that Tuberous-rooted Begonias are good house plants. Nevertheless, there are certain sections of the country where they grow beautifully; so we are including them for this reason. Normally they are grown for outdoor planting in shady locations, where their large and colorful flowers are particularly appreciated.

Tuberous-rooted Begonias blossom during the summer months, and their flowers are among the most beautiful of the season. Almost every color except blue or purple may be found in a collection of Tuberous-rooted Begonias. I especially enjoy their pastel shades of peach, salmon, and pale yellow, though you may prefer the brilliant or deep reds, the bright yellows and oranges, or the crisp whites.

Most Tuberous Begonias are upright-growing plants, usually not over one and a half feet tall, but there are trailing varieties also, which grow beautifully in hanging baskets on shaded patios, or when planted on the front edge of a window box in a north or east exposure.

Tuberous-rooted Begonias must have cool temperatures with high humidity to do well, and they must also have protection from the sun. Tubers are usually started into growth in a mixture of peat moss and sand in March or April and are then potted up singly as soon as new growth starts. Begonias like a soil composed of two parts light loam, two parts peat moss, and one part cow manure. They are heavy feeders. As they grow, it is well to feed them every ten days with a mild complete fertilizer in liquid form, applied in the place of one daily watering.

If you buy bulbs and start your own plants, do not economize on them but buy the largest and best you can afford. It is these that will produce the exhibition-type flowers expected from Tuberous-rooted Begonias.

Along in early autumn Tuberous-rooted Begonias begin their rest period. You may leave them in the ground until they are nipped by frost. Then lift them and store them over winter in dry peat moss as close to 40 degrees as you can manage. Start them another spring with full expectations of flowers as good, or better, than you had the first season.

Christmas Cactus

Almost everyone who likes house plants has, or wishes he had, a Christmas Cactus. They are among the easiest of house plants to grow, yet a great many flower lovers say that they cannot make their plants blossom. Perhaps this is true because in their minds the word *Cactus* means "burning desert sands." The Christmas Cactus, known botanically as *Zygocactus truncatus*, is not a desert plant at all. It comes from high in the treetops of moist Brazilian jungles, where it gains a foothold in the leaf-filled crotches of trees.

Now that we know something of the plant's background we can easily adjust our thinking to suit its needs. A Christmas Cactus does not want full sun at any time. Instead, it likes a location where there is an abundance of filtered light, such as suits African Violets or Gloxinias. Being from a tropical land, it enjoys warm household temperatures and fairly high humidity. It is important, also, that it receive ample moisture at all times. It has been established by careful experiments that Christmas Cacti do not have to be "dried off" before they will blossom. On the contrary, flower buds are initiated by cool temperatures, rather than drying. At night temperatures of 55 degrees to 65 degrees buds form in the short days of autumn and continue to mature so that the majority of plants flower about Christmas time. Some plants will blossom a month earlier, or even two months later, but no matter when they appear the brilliant red flowers are welcome additions to a window sill garden.

A highly organic soil, made up of two parts light loam, two parts peat moss, and one part cow manure, will make Christmas Cacti thrive. In addition, during the months when they are in active growth, they appreciate an occasional feeding with a complete house-plant fertilizer.

There are variations among Christmas Cacti, such as the Crab Cactus, which get their names from minor stem-leaf differences. You may even find plants which have been grafted onto other Cacti to give them height, for the true Christmas Cactus is a trailing plant. In any case, they all respond to the same cultural conditions.

Kalanchoes

Perhaps the first thing I should do is to tell you how to pronounce the name of this plant. It is called "kal-an-ko'ee." Kalanchoes are offered by florists from Christmas time until late March or early April. The plants are very attractive and last a long while in blossom. Their compact nature makes them ideal window sill subjects.

The type most often seen is a dwarf, red-flowered variety known as Tom Thumb. This Kalanchoe rarely grows over eight or nine inches tall, more commonly six inches or so. The flowers are brick red and are borne in thick clusters on the tops of the plants, so profusely as to nearly hide the leaves.

During winter months Kalanchoes should be given a sunny spot in which to grow, although florists give them filtered light during the summer months. Keep the soil beneath Kalanchoes on the dry side, barely moist rather than wet. I also suggest that you water them from beneath by pouring water into a saucer, rather than around the crowns of the plants.

Although Kalanchoes are perennials, they never seem to do well another season because of poor light conditions and excessive heat in most homes. I advise discarding them when the flowering period has passed. While you have them no fertilizer need be applied.

You might like to know that Kalanchoes grow in tropical parts of Africa and Asia. The ancestors of the one mentioned above came from Madagascar.

Jerusalem Cherry

If, along about Christmas time, you have seen plants in flower shops covered with what appear to be tiny oranges one half inch in diameter, then you know what a Jerusalem Cherry looks like. This same plant is also known as Cleveland Cherry. Either name is allowable.

Jerusalem Cherries are inexpensive pot plants, and if conditions are right, they will be attractive in the home for many weeks. They should be given full sunlight and should never be allowed to dry out, or the fruit and leaves will fall. It is known that Jerusalem Cherries are extremely sensitive to gas in homes. If you have kept your plant well watered and given it plenty of light, yet it dropped its fruit overnight, suspect a tiny gas leak.

Jerusalem Cherries are known botanically as *Solanum pseudo-capsicum* and are members of the Nightshade family, as are both Potatoes and Eggplant. The orange fruit is poisonous and should be kept out of reach of small children. The plants are annuals and should be thrown away when no longer attractive.

Ornamental Peppers

As an especially interesting small pot plant during late autumn or at Christmas time, you might try a plant of Ornamental Pepper. The fruit is entirely edible, but extremely pungent, and is borne above the leaves of the somewhat flat-topped plants. It is not uncommon to see tiny white flowers and white, purple, and red fruit all on a plant at the same time. They are very colorful and real conversation pieces.

Grow them on sunny window sills at as cool a temperature as you can, and keep the soil beneath them moist. It is not necessary to feed them, and since they are annuals, or nearly so, it is wise to discard them after they have outlived their usefulness.

Christmas Begonias

Like popular songs, plants come into fashion and then, in time, slip off the list of favorites. For some reason I have never been able to fathom, the Christmas Begonia is in a cycle of waning popularity. The first time you see a Christmas Begonia in full flower, its deep pink blossoms completely enveloping the plant, you too will wonder why it should ever lose its place to another.

There are several varieties of Christmas Begonias, all more or less alike. They are hybrids descended from plants brought originally from the island of Socotra in the Indian Ocean, thus giving the plants the botanical name *Begonia socotrana*.

One might almost say that a Christmas Begonia blossoms itself to death, for when the flowers have gone the plant is not worth trying to keep as a house plant. When you get a Christmas Begonia give it a well-lighted spot and keep it as cool as you can. The soil should stay moist. Plants do not have to be fed while in flower.

Miniature or Fairy Roses

It would not be correct to say that Fairy Roses are regularly available at flower shops, yet they are so desirable and unusual when grown as house plants that they deserve mention nevertheless. Imagine, if you can, Rosebushes complete with flowers, yet only six inches tall! The charm of such plants is undeniable, and their rarity and diminutiveness make them real conversation pieces. A young plant, a true Rosebush in all respects, can easily be hidden under a teacup!

It should be noted that miniature Roses are not the result of the manipulation of man, but are true dwarfs, their tiny stature being one of the factors in their genetic background. Nowadays there are numerous varieties of Fairy Roses grown with such intriguing names as Pixie, Twinkles, Tom Thumb, Bo Peep, Baby Gold Star, Midget, Tinker Bell, and Cinderella, but most of these fascinating plants are sold by color only, such as red, pink, yellow, and white. Most varieties are double flowering and represent lovely variations in shading, especially among the pink-flowering forms. It is interesting to note that one of the original forms known as *Rosa rouletti* was found many years ago growing in window boxes in a Swiss village. Upon inquiry it was learned that no one knew where it had come from, but residents of the town said that their people had grown this type of Rose for centuries!

Miniature Roses are usually available as dormant plants in the autumn or as started plants in January. Bare-root dormant plants received in autumn should be potted into rich soil containing about one fourth cow manure. Place them in a cool place, preferably outdoors where they can complete their rest period under normal conditions. A cold frame is ideal, since it provides protection from extremes of temperature.

After Christmas bring the plants into a room where the temperature is about 60 degrees and place them where they will get the maximum amount of light. Prune out weak growth and cut back the tops about one half. Daily syringing will help to encourage the initiation of new growth. Within a few weeks your plants will reward you with delicate miniature flowers about the size of a nickel.

Protect the plant foliage from insects and mildew with a Rose dust as you would outdoor Roses. Bear in mind constantly that the most limiting factor in growing them indoors is poor light. Choose your brightest spot for them.

When weather is mild they may be planted outdoors, where they will be found to be quite hardy, or the plants may be allowed to remain in the pots and be returned to the house again in the autumn. During the entire season of active growth, feed them once a month with a mild solution of a complete house-plant fertilizer.

Dish gardens

These brief notes about dish gardens are included simply because so many people do not know how to water them properly. Do not try to water a dish garden by sprinkling moisture on its surface. Submerge the entire dish garden gently under water in a pail or basin until all air bubbles cease rising. Then lift the garden out, and set it on its side for twenty minutes or so to let excess moisture drain out of the soil. Usually one such watering a week is ample.

Sometimes people ask what to do with dish gardens when the plants become overgrown. The answer is to take the plants out, pot them up separately, and continue to enjoy them as house plants. Most of the species encountered in dish gardens are very tough and well suited to growing in the average home.

CHAPTER XVII

Summer Care of House Plants

A summer in the country

House plants that have survived the winter months on a window sill are often less than robust by the time warm weather arrives. A vacation outdoors, where they can have an abundance of fresh air and light, will usually improve their health to the point where they can begin a new winter's sojourn with renewed vitality. Summer care of house plants implies that they will have the benefit of real attention to their needs during this period. A summer outdoors is not worthy to be called summer care if the plants are simply put outside at the mercy of the elements and left to shift for themselves.

All thought of putting house plants outside should be deferred until the weather is mild, both day and night. Plants that have been indoors are extremely tender when compared to outdoor plants. Their leaves are thinner and not as strong, and they are very easily damaged by the sun or wind. We should strive to make their change of environment as gentle as possible so as not to cause a check in their growth. Certain plants should not go outside. African Violets and Gloxinias, for example, with their tender fuzzy leaves, are much more adapted to house conditions than they are to the vagaries of outdoor living.

Moment of decision

When you get ready to put your plants outside, inspect them with a critical eye and decide whether they are all really worth trying to coax through the summer. Some may be too large for your house but useful as a source of cuttings. Some plants will benefit by having a severe pruning that will act as a rejuvenator so that new growth will be compact and robust. Others may be awkward and gawky and altogether worthless. Do not waste a summer's effort on them.

Thoughts on potting

You must decide which plants need to be repotted. It is possible that most of them should have fresh soil, even though they may be repotted into the same pots in which they have been growing. This brings up an interesting phase of horticulture too seldom practiced in this country. For centuries the Japanese have grown plants in pots under a system called Bonsai, which in its finest sense enables plants to live for decades in tiny containers. An adaptation of this method is extremely useful in growing many house plants in this country. While the Japanese prune off part of the roots of their plants and further dwarf them by reducing their tops as well, we can accomplish somewhat the same idea by washing off old soil from roots and repotting in fresh soil. At the same time a judicious pruning of top growth will tend to keep plants more shapely and within bounds. Plants that we want to grow larger are best repotted at this season in larger containers so that they may make their growth during the summer season.

One of the essential elements of summer care of house plants out of doors is to be certain that the roots of the plants stay within the confines of flowerpots. If they are planted out in the garden or plunged incorrectly, the roots will wander far and wide and you will never get them back into the flowerpots again. In order to keep roots confined, you would do well to keep fertile soil in the pots and to set the pots on a layer of at least three or four inches of coarse gravel so that the roots will not have the tendency to steal out of the drainage holes in search of food or moisture. It is a good idea to give the pots a turn once in a while so as to discourage ranging roots.

Summer home

Choose a special site for each type of plant in relationship to its demand for light. Sun lovers should get full sunshine; others, moderate or deeper shade depending on their needs. Prepare the spot for your plants by digging out a sunken bed ten inches or so deep and placing a layer of coarse gravel three or four inches deep on the bottom. The depth of the gravel under each pot should be such that, when the pots are set on it, their rims will be about one inch above the normal soil level. Fill in around the pots with moist peat moss or soil. Peat moss is much to be preferred, since it not only holds a great deal of moisture but also is free of weed seeds, and there will be little or no weeding necessary around the pots during the summer season. Separate the plants widely enough so that they can grow without crowding.

Summer is the ideal time to clean up infestations of bugs, since you can use the garden sprayer on them. Use Malathion according to manufacturer's directions. Spray thoroughly, going after the bugs on the undersides of the leaves especially. When watering, remember that you have an excellent opportunity to help your plants by using the force of water pressure to wash insects off leaves and to give the leaves a real bath.

The last consideration of summer care is quite like the first; that is, return your plants to winter quarters in your home before nights get so cool as to curtail their growth. At this time survey them once more to see how they have come through the summer. Be ruthless with the weaklings because a winter window sill makes a poor plant hospital. Plants that cannot regain their vigor during a summer's vacation out of doors will never be satisfactory in your house.

CHAPTER XVIII

On Being Your Own Doctor

Sign language

How are you at playing doctor? Under the care of each plant I have tried to tell you about the troubles which sometimes beset them. Now I shall state in general terms the place the three major fertilizer elements play in good plant health and how you can learn to interpret your plants' needs. You will find an analysis of every fertilizer stated on each package as a group of three numerals, such as 4–8–4, 12–12–12, or 10–6–2. The first figure in each case refers to the percentage of nitrogen, the second, of phosphoric acid, and the third, of water-soluble potash that the fertilizer contains.

Nitrogen is associated with deep green color, and plants lacking it have uniformly yellowish-green foliage. Plants having an optimum amount of nitrogen grow rapidly and have beautiful dark green leaves.

Phosphoric acid is essential to the new growth of plants, and in its absence plants often stay dark green but refuse to grow.

The role potash plays is not clearly understood. Plants lacking it have a tendency toward dying at the edges of leaves. Scientists think that one of the most important functions of potash may be that of a catalyst, whereby it helps other elements to become assimilated.

Beyond these three there are many so-called minor elements. They are minor in the sense that only a small amount of each needs to be present, but even these small amounts are essential to most plants. Boron, copper, iron, magnesium, manganese, silicon, sulphur, and zinc are considered to be minor elements.

A good physician knows that a given amount of medicine is helpful, but too much may be lethal. The same formula holds for plants as well as for warm-blooded creatures. If your fertilizer directions say to use a teaspoonful to a gallon, do not double the amount because it does not look strong enough!

It is well to remember that everything which enters through the roots of a plant must be in liquid form. The reason that inorganic or chemical fertilizers work swiftly is that they dissolve in water relatively fast. Organic fertilizers, such as cow manure or bone meal, have to be acted upon by soil bacteria and broken down to their essential elements before a plant can use them. They are slow acting, but their benefits last a long while. Organic fertilizers rarely release their nutrients fast enough to injure tender roots.

While we are talking about fertilizers it is well to remember that sick plants or newly transplanted ones must be fed with very mild fertilizers compared with what established plants can use. Treat them with gentleness as you would any convalescent.

Soil pH

Soil is said to be neutral when its reading is 7 on the pH scale. Below 7, soils become increasingly acid and above 7, increasingly alkaline. Most house plants grow best in soils that have a pH of 5.5 to 7. Acid-loving plants, such as Azaleas and Gardenias, prefer soil testing 4.5 to 5.5. When a plant is growing in soil that is not acid enough it signals its difficulty by sending forth pale green leaves with dark green veins. When this condition exists, water the plants with a solution of one ounce of iron sulphate to two gallons of water. The *p*H of soils can be changed from acid to alkaline by the application of lime.

Home on the range!

Are bugs finding green pastures among your house plants? With all the new insecticides on the market each year it should be an easy matter to overwhelm them. Many of the sprays are designed to control specific insects, and it is necessary to read labels carefully and to follow directions to the letter. As an all-purpose spray for house plants in summer quarters you can use a material known as Malathion, giving them a thorough covering when you put them outside for the summer and again a few days before returning them to the house. It cannot be stated too clearly that you should read all the directions on the labels before using any spray materials on your plants. Often a close reading will disclose that certain plants are intolerant of the material.

Test run

One of the most exasperating things that can happen to persons trying to grow plants in their homes is to have them drop their flowers almost overnight and not grow any new ones. The chief villain, and a most elusive one, is gas. Manufactured gas is by far (500 to 500,000 times) more deadly to plants than natural gas. One part of manufactured gas per million parts of air in twenty-four hours will cause some plants to drop their flowers and others to hang their leaves in a drooping position.

Some of the finest florists in the world have been accused of selling old flowers or poor plants because there happened to be tiny gas leaks in some of their customers' homes. A freshly cut Carnation will close its petals up and "go to sleep" in a few hours when gas is present. Under normal conditions it will stay lovely for nearly a week.

If you suspect gas injury to your plants, buy a Carnation and see how it behaves. If it wants to slumber, then call the gas company!

CHAPTER XIX

A Flower Lover's Postscript

Our story about house plants has been told, but there are still some items of lasting horticultural interest which I feel should be included in this book.

All leaves are golden

I never sniff the scent of burning autumn leaves, but I wish I had room for a bigger compost pile. The leaves which drift from trees each fall are filled with goodness for your garden, not only for the food value in them, but also for the value of their organic matter in improving the tilth of your soil. *Good tilth* are the magical words gardeners use, but rarely define. They imply a combination of those factors which have been found essential to healthy plant growth. No other element is more essential to good tilth than an optimum amount of organic matter. Organic matter improves all kinds of soils. It helps light soils hold moisture, and it lightens and aerates heavy soils. Organic matter helps to keep soils from washing away and improves their capacity to hold water, which will sustain plants in times of drought.

Nowadays it is almost impossible to obtain barnyard manure for gardens. It is well for you to know that properly prepared compost is a near equal in value to manure for your plants. In making a compost pile, combine chemicals with whatever organic material is available, leaves, grass clippings, straw, or any plant refuse that is not diseased. Choose a secluded corner in your garden for your compost pile. Make it flat-topped so that it will catch rain water, for moisture is necessary for decay to take place.

Decomposition is aided not only by keeping the pile wet but also by adding small amounts of a complete inorganic fertilizer, such as 5–8–7, and ground limestone to the pile as it is built. A mixture of ten pounds of fertilizer and two and a half pounds of ground limestone should be added to the pile at the rate of one pint to two bushels of dry plant material.

Keep the compost pile moist and turn it over with a garden fork two or three times a year. It takes about six months to produce usable compost, and the longer it decays, the better it is. Try using sifted compost in place of peat moss in some of your potting mixtures, and see how your plants thrive.

Longer life for cut flowers

Possibly in no other phase of horticulture will you find so many divergent views as there are concerning the care of cut flowers. Over the years any number of home remedies have been suggested, including the use of vinegar, sugar, aspirin, and pennies, cutting stems under water, and a host of other ideas. It is interesting to note that when these theories are subjected to the cold light of science, most of them prove to be either of little value or an actual detriment to the flowers.

In order to explain the reasons that I suggest certain procedures in caring for cut flowers, I should like to review briefly some of the processes which take place within living plants. Growing plants manufacture food in their leaves during daylight hours and use part of it to keep themselves growing during the hours of darkness. Flowers cut in late afternoon, therefore, have a greater store of food in their tissues than those cut early in the morning; thus they last longer.

Another factor to be considered is that flowers start to

wilt the moment they are cut, whether they show it or not; therefore it is extremely important that they be placed in warm water as soon as possible. Notice that I said *warm* water, for that is often the key to satisfactory cut flowers. No doubt, you remember as a child picking wildflowers, only to have them become discouragingly wilted before you could get them home. Rarely did they revive either because they were given a drink of ice-cold water when in reality they needed warm water. All life processes move forward at an accelerated pace as temperatures rise, and plants are no exceptions. If we want wilted flowers to revive, we should put them in warm water, which the stems can absorb quickly. The ideal procedure to perk up wilted flowers is to cut the stems, plunge them in deep warm water (about 100 degrees), and then place them in a cool room. In cool temperatures the tops of the flowers tend to hold in moisture while the warm water is quickly taken in from below. Within a very short time the cells are full of moisture, and the flowers can hold their heads up unassisted.

When you arrange flowers for yourself, use warm water even if the flowers are fresh from your florist. All too many florists have been accused of selling old flowers simply because their customers arranged their flowers in cold water and placed them in hot rooms. Of course, the tops lost moisture to the hot atmosphere faster than the stems could absorb it, and they wilted; obvious conclusion, the florist sent old flowers! An old florist friend of mine once said, "It may be that the florist business *is* a bed of roses because there surely are some thorns!"

You will find that almost all florists cut the stems of their flowers with a sharp knife perhaps because it is a faster way to shorten them than to use shears. Some contend that shears squeeze the ends of stems, reducing their ability to absorb water, but scientific tests have shown that one method has no practical advantage over the other except to satisfy the whims of the user.

The one accepted way to prolong the life of cut flowers is to use one of the commercial cut-flower preservatives in the water. The formulas of these preparations are based on two principles: first, the fewer bacteria that survive in the water, the slower will be the decay action on the stems; and second, since the flowers are severed from their parent plants, food, in a usable form, will tend to keep the flowers alive. Cut-flower preparations have been given thousands of impartial tests by laboratories which do everything possible to arrive at accurate evaluations. Tests on any given flower have been repeated time and time again to remove the element of chance.

Interestingly enough, it has been clearly shown that some flowers are not helped, no matter what is done for them. There are inherent factors over which we have no control at present. As an example, Daylilies were given that name because each of their flowers lasts only one day. Men have not been able to make an elixir which will change nature's plan. Similarly, all flowers have a certain built-in time schedule. By the use of these products, however, the beauty life of Carnations can be extended from about a week or less to over two weeks. Chrysanthemums, Delphiniums, Roses, and Snapdragons will last about one fourth longer with a cut-flower preparation in the water than when arranged in plain water. When one of these products is used, it is not necessary or advisable to change the water, but simply to add more as the flowers use it up.

The cut-flower life of many plants is more influenced by the conditions under which they are grown than any other one factor. Sweet Peas, for instance, growing in cool, sunny weather will hold their flowers very well, but after a series of dull, cloudy days they become extremely short lived.

Plants whose stems exude a white or sticky sap, such as Poppies and Poinsettias, as well as some hollow-stemmed flowers, of which Dahlias are examples, need special treatment when used as cut flowers. The ends of the stems must be cauterized in order that the cells may not become clogged with dried sap. This may be accomplished by searing them over a flame or by dipping them in rapidly boiling water. A candle flame is easy to use. Cut the stem the length you need for your arrangement, sear it over the flame, then put it in the vase.

Over the years Roses have maintained their popularity despite the fact that a great many people feel that they are not as satisfactory as they should be. Complaints have ranged all the way from the criticism that some Rose flowers will not open at all to the objection that certain Roses open and fade overnight. There is no question but that the longevity of Roses as cut flowers varies with different varieties as well as the conditions under which they are grown. This factor is a built-in one over which flower buyers have no control. Thus one group of Roses will often last longer than another, although given similar treatment. Sunny weather encourages firm-textured, long-lasting flowers, while cloudy skies have an opposite effect.

Rosebuds must reach a certain stage of maturity before they are cut. This is another variable associated with the difference in growth habits of different varieties. Perhaps you have had Roses which refused to open. Sometimes, though not necessarily, the fault lies in cutting the buds before they have advanced to the stage where they can continue to open. Florists call such buds "green."

Some Roses appear to be lovely when received from a florist, but within a short while the flower stems just below the blossoms weaken, and the flowers hang their heads. This frustrating situation is usually not the florist's fault, but comes about because the flowers are not able to absorb water fast enough to keep from wilting. To obviate this situation, recut stems before arranging Roses, arrange them in warm water to which a cut-flower preservative has been added, and see that they do not go into too hot a room. Wilting is always a sign that flowers are not getting enough water; it does not always mean that they are old! Wilted roses will usually revive overnight if stems are recut and submerged in warm water up to the flower heads. If you do not have a deep enough container, lay them in warm water in the kitchen sink.

Chrysanthemums are among the longest-lasting and loveliest flowers of any season, but they, too, often have a way of wilting which discourages those who do not know how to remedy the situation. The large-flowered Mums are particularly susceptible to wilting. Usually the leaves wilt while the flower heads remain more or less upright. A common treatment is to remove most of the foliage so that the cut stems will not have to support so much leaf area. An old florist recipe calls for adding a few drops of essence of peppermint to the water. (See your druggist.) This seems to have a remarkable effect toward reducing the wilting of Chrysanthemums. You will find it advantageous to split or crush the ends of Chrysanthemum stems to help them take up moisture. As with other flowers, arrange Chrysanthemums in warm water.

During the Christmas season most of us feel that Holly is a particularly appropriate plant to arrange for a lasting display. Experience soon shows that Holly branches dry out very quickly as some have found to their sorrow. Be sure your branches are fresh from the florist. Make new cuts at the bases of the branches and arrange them in a

vase filled with warm water. It will be helpful at this time
to set your arrangement in a very cool place for several
hours to allow the branches to fill their cells with moisture.
It is interesting to note that many Holly growers protect
their cut branches from drying in transit by spraying them
with an invisible coating of a waxlike material. This benefit
carries over to the consumer by making Holly last longer
in the house.

The year without a summer

Many years ago parts of our country experienced what
was called a year without a summer. Freezing weather cut
down gardens in mid-July. During every month of the year
there were frosts which kept crops from maturing. There
were no flowers in the land. This story is told to bring into
focus the fact that, at this very moment, there are many
thousands of persons who, to all intents and purposes, are
experiencing a year without a summer in their own lives.
These are the unfortunate among us who have to spend
days and weeks, even years, in hospital beds or confined at
home.

We like to be thought of as a generous people, and we
give of our money to finance projects in distant parts of the
world, yet some of us forget the little kindnesses which
make life worth living. Do something close to home. Plan
to visit the sick and the lonely regularly, and carry a few
flowers with you. See the joy you bring to another by giving
of yourself. Perhaps you could volunteer to arrange flowers and care for pot plants at your local hospital and relieve
nurses of that extra chore. Do something yourself, if it is
only to bring a single flower to a shut-in. See that no one
in your town has a year without a summer.

INDEX